Practical English Writing Skills

A Complete Guide to Writing in English

Mona Scheraga

National Textbook Company
NTC a division of *NTC Publishing Group* • Lincolnwood, Illinois USA

To my mother and father,

Jean and Ben Liechenstein,

whose faith and encouragement have made it all possible

Contents

Acknowledgments

Working with Becky Rauff, my editor on this project, has been a special privilege. Her patience, insight, and expertise cannot be overestimated. The thousands of students who passed through my classes in over twenty-five years of teaching deserve a special thanks. Each, in turn, helped fine-tune my understanding of the infinite dimensions of the teaching/learning process. To my husband, Murray, for being confidant and adviser, artist and proofreader, and chief cook and pot scrubber during the writing of this text, go the thanks of an extremely grateful if sometimes neglectful wife.

I really must thank the profession, English as a second/foreign language, for the friends I've made in the field. To Professor Alice Jiménez, Special Assistant to the Secretary of Education of Puerto Rico and a very special friend, my thanks for her incisive comments and suggestions as she read portions of the work in progress. For their advice and support, too, go thanks to Dr. Gladys Nussenbaum and Connie Attanasio.

I am grateful to Northwestern University, Evanston, Illinois, for allowing us to reprint a Northwestern Application for Admission, to William Paterson College, Wayne, New Jersey, for allowing us to reprint a William Paterson College Application for Admission, and to TOPS Business Forms, Wheeling, Illinois, for permission to use two of their job application forms. Special thanks, too, to Kathy Blattner for allowing me to use her fascinating term paper on the Amish.

I would like to acknowledge all the people I have worked with and learned from over the years. I am not unaware of how lucky I am to have been exposed to so many meaningful experiences in and out of the classroom.

Introduction

Practical English Writing Skills is a guide to developing the writing skills we all need to function and succeed in our everyday lives—at home, on the job, and in school. Unlike any other writing text, this book addresses the simplest and yet most essential skills such as taking a message and writing a thank-you note, then builds to more advanced skills such as writing a résumé and making a bibliography. Along the way, each type of writing is discussed and explained in a straightforward, helpful way, treating the everyday tasks with as much respect as the more academic skills.

Practical English Writing Skills is for high school, junior college, and adult education limited English proficient students. It is also for English as a foreign language students planning to live/work/function in an English-speaking environment, and for the many native speakers of English who need help mastering a variety of basic writing skills. The format of the book also makes *Practical English Writing Skills* suitable for independent study: for students who want to improve their writing skills on their own without a formal language program.

This book covers all kinds of writing, from taking phone messages to writing term papers, and it provides the following for each type of writing:

1. A **Rationale** for doing this type of writing;

2. a list of the **Materials Needed;**

3. the **Skills Involved;**

4. **Important Vocabulary;**

5. an **Example** of the kind of writing to be practiced;

6. a step-by-step **Procedure** for doing the writing; and

7. a **Practice** activity: a real-life task that involves the kind of writing that's been discussed.

In addition, most of the lessons include an evaluation process to measure the success of the written practice.

Practical English Writing Skills is meant to be used as it best suits the user. Therefore, you can start at page one and follow through to the end; start in the middle and work backward and forward at will; or even start with the last chapter, if that's the one you need immediately. No matter where you begin, you will find that *Practical English Writing Skills* is not only a guide but also an easy reference book, much the same as your dictionary is. You can turn to this book anytime for information about whatever type of writing you need to do. The book was written with your needs in mind. Enjoy.

UNIT ONE

NOTES AND MESSAGES

CHAPTER 1
Leaving a Note

There are many times we want to leave a note for someone. For example, if you're leaving home when everyone else is sleeping and you won't be back at your usual time, you might want to leave a note so no one will worry about you. If you want to remind someone to do you a favor or to call you later or to remember to meet you at a certain time, you can leave that person a note.

 Rationale

At times, it is more considerate to leave a note for someone than to disturb that person; for example, you could leave someone a note if you want that person to remember

> that you have an appointment together, or
> that you won't be home for dinner, or
> to pick up your clothes at the dry cleaners.

If you leave your message in writing, there's less chance the person will forget it—especially if that person is half asleep or busy with something else and not listening carefully. Another good time to leave a note is when you have a message for someone who isn't at home or isn't available to talk to you. When you leave a note, you can be sure that you have let the person know your message.

 Materials Needed

paper, pen or pencil

 Skills Involved

organizing thoughts; giving specific information; using correct spelling, punctuation, capitalization, and abbreviations

▷▷ Important Vocabulary

considerate thoughtful

disturb bother

do someone a favor help someone

note a short letter

organizing thoughts arranging information in a clear, logical order. A note that says *Meet me at 3 P.M. Pick up my clothes at the dry cleaners. I'll be in front of the post office* is not as clear as *Meet me at 3 P.M. in front of the post office. Please pick up my clothes at the dry cleaners first.*

pick up get

remind tell someone to remember

specific information facts and details; *at 3 P.M. in front of the post office* is specific information

▷▷ Examples

A.
> Mom,
> I won't be home until 4:30. I'm going to the library after school with Kim.
> Jean

B.
> Jean,
> I'll be at the office until 5 P.M. The soup is on the stove. Please turn the burner on low at 4:30. See you later.
> Mom

C.
> Bill,
> Please pick me up in front of Brown's Dept. Store on Main St. at 4:45 P.M. I'll be waiting outside.
> Tanya

Procedure

1. Use a piece of paper that is large enough to be seen.

2. Organize your thoughts and then write down your message.

3. Be sure your handwriting—including your signature—is easy to read, especially if there are times, addresses, or directions involved.

4. Put your note where it will be seen by the person you want to read it. If the note is for a family member, you might want to tape it to the refrigerator or on the bathroom mirror or next to the telephone.

5. Read your note again. Be sure your message is clear.

Practice

Now it's your turn.

TASK: to leave a note for someone

SITUATION: You leave the house before your brother is awake. You want him to pick you up at your friend's house at 6 P.M. Think about what he needs to know, and write a note to leave for him. *Be sure to give him specific information.*

Did you remember to give your brother this information:

> your friend's name
> your friend's address and telephone number
> directions to your friend's house if he isn't familiar with the street?

If you forgot any of this important information, you may still be waiting to be picked up!

CHAPTER 2
Writing a Note

Most people don't realize how important notes are in our daily lives. Every day thousands of people write notes to thousands of others who read them, or try to. Sometimes note writers are in such a hurry that they forget to write so that others can understand their handwriting or their message. However, notes are just about the easiest thing to learn to write.

▷▷ Rationale

Most of us write many, many notes in a lifetime. If you're in school now, for example, you might write a note to explain to your teacher why you didn't do a certain homework assignment if you're too nervous to just speak to the teacher. You might want to be excused from school early one day, and if you're eighteen or older you can write your own note explaining why. Another type of note might even be a short letter of apology to someone you're too shy to face in person, such as a friend you've been rude to. If you have children, you may want to make an appointment to see your child's teacher, or you may need to write an "excuse" for your child's absence or a note requesting that your child be excused from some activity on a particular day.

▷▷ Materials Needed

unlined stationery, envelope, pen

▷▷ Skills Involved

organizing thoughts; giving specific information; using correct spelling, punctuation, capitalization, and abbreviations

Important Vocabulary

absence being away from someplace; for example, being away from school

apology saying you're sorry

closing a word or phrase used to end a letter. The closing is found just above the writer's signature and is always followed by a comma.

copy something that is exactly like something else; for example, if you want to have proof that you have written a certain note, you should make a copy of it to keep for yourself

excuse reason given for something; for example, many schools want a written excuse when a student returns from an absence

indented form a format for writing letters in which the first line of each paragraph is placed farther in from the margin than the salutation

margin the space that is left empty on the top, bottom, and sides of a page containing a note or other writing

modified block form a format for writing letters in which the margins are the same from the first line to the end. Nothing is indented. A blank space is left between paragraphs.

note a short letter

salutation the greeting in a letter, usually beginning with *Dear* followed by a person's name

Examples

A. Indented Form

right margin

top margin —

salutation —

January, 11 19—

Dear Mr. Garcia,

Please excuse my daughter, Connie Ballou, at 1:45 P.M. today. We have an appointment with Dr. Anne Ache at 2 P.M. It was the only appointment we could get. Thank you.

left margin

closing —

Sincerely,

Mrs. Jane Ballou

bottom margin —

B. Modified Block Form

March 15, 19—

Dear Marco,

I'm sorry I was so rude yesterday. I was nervous because of the big math test. When you asked to borrow my homework, I really got angry because I had worked so hard on it. Please call me later.

Your friend,
Ashok

top margin

salutation

right margin

closing

bottom margin

left margin

▶ Procedure

1. Use a piece of unlined stationery. If your stationery is the fold-over kind, write on the inside.

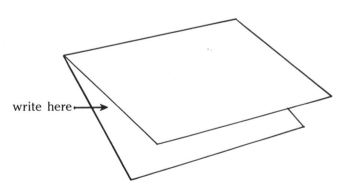

write here

2. Leave a margin on all four sides of the stationery.

3. Write the date in the upper right-hand corner.

June 9, 19—

4. Leave some space below the date. Then, starting at the left-hand margin, write *Dear* and the name of the person you're writing to. This is called the *salutation*. It is the greeting at the beginning of any note

or letter. The first letter of the first word and the names of any people in the salutation should be capitalized. Put a comma after the salutation.

> *June 9, 19—*
>
> *Dear Ms. Wang,*

5. Below the salutation, begin your message. You can use modified block form or you can indent the first line.

> *June 9, 19—*
>
> *Dear Ms. Wang,*
> *I'm sorry I didn't give you my homework today, but I was working on the floor and my dog came over and stepped on it and messed it all up. I didn't want to give you a dirty paper, but I promise I won't do my homework on the floor anymore.*

6. Under the message, on the right, end your note with a word or phrase that shows respect and how you feel. *Sincerely* is a good word to use because it says that you really mean what you say. This word or phrase is called the *closing*. The first word of the closing should be capitalized. Put a comma after the closing.

7. Sign your name below the closing. When you write to a teacher, it's a good idea to use your complete name.

> *Sincerely,*
> *Filomena Danang*

The finished note should look something like this:

June 9, 19—

Dear Ms. Wang,

I'm sorry I didn't give you my homework today, but I was working on the floor and my dog came over and stepped on it and messed it all up. I didn't want to give you a dirty paper, but I promise I won't do my homework on the floor anymore.

Sincerely,
Filomena Danang

8. Put the note in an envelope and write the person's name in the middle of the envelope.

Ms. Wang

Practice

Now it's your turn.

TASK: to write a note to someone

SITUATION: You want to leave school early tomorrow because you have to go take your driver's test. Write a note to the school principal, asking to be excused. Remember the form:

Remember to write carefully so the other person can read your handwriting easily. After you finish writing, read your note again to make sure you haven't made any mistakes.

CHAPTER 3
Writing a Thank-You Note

We write thank-you notes for many reasons at different times in our lives. For example, you have just had a surprise birthday party. Guests brought gifts to your party, and out-of-town relatives sent gifts by mail. You thank people at the party, but you also want to write each one a note afterwards, naming the particular gift he or she gave you. Writing a thank-you note shows you appreciate the time, effort, and money spent by someone who brought or sent you a present. Of course, you could make phone calls or buy thank-you notes that say it already; but since someone thought enough of you to make or buy a gift for you, you want to show the same thoughtfulness.

Another time you might write a thank-you note is when someone has done something special for you. You want to show your appreciation, so you write a note thanking the person for being so kind.

Another occasion for writing thank-you notes might be when someone close to you has died. Friends visit you to help you in your time of sorrow. Later, you send notes thanking them for caring.

▷▷ Rationale

Someone has taken the time, energy, and money to buy or make a gift for you or to show you in some nice way that you are special. To express your appreciation, you take the time and energy to thank the person with a short note, especially if (1) you received the person's gift by mail, (2) you received many gifts at the same time and you want to let the giver know you are aware of and appreciate his or her particular gift, or (3) the note is in response to a kindness or special favor.

▷▷ Materials Needed

unlined stationery, matching envelope, postage stamp, pen, dictionary to check spelling, correct name and complete address of gift giver, information about kind of gift received

Skills Involved

writing simple sentences; using correct punctuation, spelling, and capitalization; expressing thanks; showing gratitude by mentioning specific gift given and something special about it

Important Vocabulary

closing a word or phrase used to end a letter. The closing is found just above the writer's signature and is always followed by a comma.

come in handy be useful

grateful thankful, appreciative

indented form a format for writing letters in which the first line of each paragraph is placed farther in from the margin than the salutation

margin the space that is left empty on the top, bottom, and sides of a page containing a note or other writing

matching envelope an envelope that is the right size and color for the stationery you are using

modified block form a format for writing letters in which the margins are the same from the first line to the end. Nothing is indented. A blank space is left between paragraphs.

note a short letter

return address the name and address of the person sending a note or letter

salutation the greeting in a letter, usually beginning with *Dear* followed by a person's name

Examples

A. Modified Block Form

top margin ────────────────

December 29, 19—

salutation ────────────────
Dear John,

left margin ────────────────
Thank you for the beautiful sweater. I really love the color.

closing ────────────────
Sincerely,
Marsha

bottom margin ────────────────

right margin

B. Indented Form

December 27, 19— .... top margin

Dear Marsha, ... salutation

.... right margin

Thank you for the great wallet. I really needed one.

Sincerely, ... closing

John

.... bottom margin

left margin

▶ Procedure A: Writing the Letter

1. Use a piece of unlined stationery. If your stationery is the fold-over kind, write on the inside.

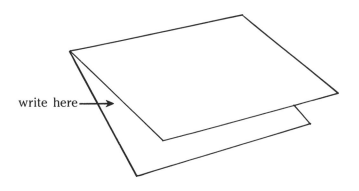

write here →

2. Leave a margin on both sides of the stationery.

3. Put the date in the upper right-hand corner.

June 11, 19—

4. Leave some space below the date. Then, starting at the left-hand margin, write *Dear* and the name of the person you're writing to. This is called the *salutation*. It is the greeting at the beginning of any note or letter. The first letter of the first word and all names in the salutation should be capitalized. Put a comma after the salutation.

June 11, 19—

Dear Aunt Sally,

5. Below the salutation, begin your message. You can use block form or you can indent the first line. Thank the person by naming the gift and telling why it's useful or what you like about it. Look at these examples.

A.

June 11, 19—

Dear Aunt Sally,
Thank you for the beautiful sweater. I love the color and I know it will keep me warm this winter.

B.

Thank you for the book. I can't wait to read it.

C.

Thank you for the check. I know it will come in handy.

6. Under the message, on the right, end your note with a word or phrase that shows how you feel. *Sincerely* is a good word to use with friends and older people. You might want to say something stronger— for example, *With love* or *Fondly*—if you're writing to someone you're very close to. This word or phrase is called the *closing*. The first word of the closing should be capitalized. Put a comma after the closing.

Sincerely,
Jim

7. Sign your name below the closing. Since you're writing to a friend or family member, your first name is all that's necessary.

This is what your letter might look like:

> *June 11, 19—*
>
> *Dear Aunt Sally,*
>
> *Thank you for the beautiful sweater. I love the color. I know it will keep me warm this winter.*
>
> > *Sincerely,*
> > *Jim*

 Practice A

Now it's your turn.

TASK: to write a thank-you note

SITUATION: You have received a present from your cousin, who lives in another state. You want to let him know you received the gift and are very grateful. Remember the form:

<pre>
                              _____

    _____,

    _____

    _____

                              _____,

                              _____
</pre>

Remember to write with a pen and to read your note after you finish writing it to make sure you haven't made mistakes.

 Procedure B: Addressing the Envelope

Now you must address the envelope. It is extremely important to use the correct name, address, and any special codes for the city, state, or country you're writing to.

1. Put your name and address in the upper left-hand corner of the envelope so that if the letter cannot be delivered for some reason, it will be returned to you. This is called the *return address*.

2. In the center of the envelope, write the name and address of the person you have written to. Put the name first, the number and street below that, and the city, state, and zip code on a third line. If there is an apartment number, it can go on the second line after the street name. If the letter is going to another country, be sure to put the name of the country on a fourth line.

3. Put a postage stamp in the upper right-hand corner. Be sure to use the right amount of postage or the letter will not be delivered.

The finished envelope should look like this:

Jim Brown
425 E. Grant St. Apt. 11B
Lincoln, ND 74583

Ms. Sally Saucer
411 Ashburn Terrace
Denver, CO 54321

▶ Practice B

Now it's your turn.

TASK: to address an envelope

CHAPTER 4
Taking a Message

The telephone rings. You are the only one there to answer it. The call is for someone else. You say you'll "take a message."

Rationale

If someone calls for you when you aren't home or at work and another person answers the phone, you'd probably like to know who called you, when, and why. The person for whom you're taking a message would like to know the same things.

Materials Needed

paper, pen or pencil

Skills Involved

listening comprehension; asking the right questions; taking notes; knowing how to use abbreviations

Important Vocabulary

abbreviation a shortened form of a word; for example, *Mr.* for *Mister, appt.* for *appointment*

can (may) *Can* really means "Am I able to?" *May* really means "Do I have your permission to?" However, *can* is acceptable in informal or colloquial speech when asking permission, as in "Can I take a message?"

hold on wait a minute; don't hang up the phone. This expression is often used when you want the person to wait while you get paper and pencil to take a message.

legible clear and easy to read

take a message write down what someone is telling you, usually to give to someone else

text written words

⟫ Example

Look at this conversation and pretend it is taking place over the telephone.

YOU: Hello.

LARRY HARP: Hello. May I speak to Mr. Ross, please?

YOU: I'm sorry. He's not here right now. Can (May) I take a message? (or, Would you like to leave a message?)

LARRY HARP: Yes. This is Larry Harp. I had an appointment with Mr. Ross for tomorrow morning at 9 A.M. I want to change the appointment. Please have him call me.

YOU: Would you spell your last name for me, please?

LARRY HARP: Harp. H-A-R-P as in Peter.

YOU: What's your phone number, Mr. Harp?

LARRY HARP: 555-0632.

YOU: 555-0632? Let me be sure I have the correct information. You want to change your appointment for tomorrow morning and you want Mr. Ross to call you.

LARRY HARP: Right.

YOU: Okay, I'll give him the message.

LARRY HARP: Thank you. Good-bye.

YOU: Bye.

What notes would you write down during the conversation? Look at this example:

> *Mr. Ross- Mr. Harp- 3:25 P.M. wants change appt. for tom. morn. Call 555-0632.*

Rewrite the message so Mr. Ross will understand it if you're not there to explain it:

Mr. Ross,

Mr. Harp called at 3:25 P.M. Wants to change appt. for tomorrow A.M. Call him at 555-0632.

Bill Williams

If Mr. Ross is your father, change the salutation to *Dad*, and sign your first name only.

▶ **Procedure**

1. It's important to have paper and a pen or pencil near the phone for taking messages. If you don't have any, ask the person who has called to please "hold on" while you get what you need. Don't trust your memory alone. You might forget an important part of the message, like the phone number, or you might not get to see the person to deliver the message. Here are some polite expressions you can use on the phone:

a. She's not here right now. Please hold on while I get a pen.

b. Would you like to leave a message?

c. Just one moment. I'll get a piece of paper. . . . Now, what is your message, please?

2. As you listen and take notes, use abbreviations that will be easy for you to remember when it's time to write the message out. Some easy ones include the following:

A.M.   morning

aft.   afternoon

appt.   appointment

Ave.   Avenue

Dr.   Doctor

eve.   evening

Mr. Mister

Ms. Miss

P.M. afternoon or evening (used with a number)

St. Street

w/ with

number

& and

It helps to be familiar with common abbreviations of cities, states, and countries if you have to take messages at work. Abbreviations for the days and months are also useful to know.

3. As you listen to the caller and take notes, write only the necessary words. You can always write the message over again once you have the important facts. (See the notes about the example conversation above.)

4. Don't be afraid to ask the caller to repeat information, including how to spell his or her name. If you hear letters you're not sure of, use a familiar word to identify each letter, for example, "Is that *F* as in *Frank*?"

5. Repeat the message to the caller to be sure you've got the correct information.

6. Write the message out and read it over before you leave it. Is it clear? Is it legible? Will the receiver understand it if you're not there to explain it? Messages do not have to be written in complete sentences. You can use abbreviations as long as you make the message clear.

7. Be sure to sign the message and tell what time you answered the phone.

8. Leave the message in a place where you're sure it will be seen by the appropriate person.

▶ **Practice**

Now it's your turn.

TASK: to take a telephone message for someone else

SITUATION: You are working in a store. The owner has gone out, asking you to take any messages. The telephone rings. Listen to the conversation* and take notes. What message would you leave for Mr. Patel?

---

*Your teacher will read or play the conversation for you. However, the text of the conversation is printed in Appendix A. If you are studying independently, try to find someone to read it to you so you can practice taking notes from a listening situation. If there is no one to read the conversation to you, look at the text and take notes from it, remembering that this is not quite the same as hearing the words.

Take notes here as you listen to the caller:

Write your message here:

Did your message look something like this?

> Mr. Patel,
>
> Mrs. Sung from Apt. 14L next door called at 2 P.M. You sent her the wrong order. She wants 3 cans of cola and 2 gallons of milk. She rec'd 2 cans of cola + 3 gallons of milk. I told her you'd call her at 555-8797 as soon as you came back.
>
> Naresh

Note that *and* (&) and *received* (rec'd) can be abbreviated.
Your message could be even shorter:

> Mr. Patel,
>
> Mrs. Sung, Apt. 14L next door, wants 3 cans cola, 2 gallons milk. You sent the opposite. Told her you'd call (555-8797) when you came back.
>
> Naresh
> 2 P.M. Tues.

What's important is to include the name, address, and phone number of the caller, the time of the call, and the message.

UNIT TWO

LETTERS

CHAPTER 5
Requesting a College Application

At some time in your life, you may decide you want to go to college. Your goal may be to get a degree or just to take some courses. Either way, you will have to fill out an application from the college. You can get one by writing to the college or university and requesting that an application be sent to you.

 Rationale

Different colleges have different entrance requirements, just as different jobs do. Many colleges also specialize in certain subject areas. Therefore, you may need to look at catalogs and applications from several schools to see which ones would be best for you and which ones would be most likely to accept you as a student. The easiest way to obtain the information you need is to write a short letter to the colleges of your choice, requesting an application and a catalog from each one.

 Materials Needed

unlined typing paper or stationery, envelopes, postage stamps, pen or typewriter (or word processor)

Skills Involved

organizing thoughts; giving and asking for specific information; using correct punctuation, spelling, capitalization, and abbreviations; typing or handwriting neatly

Important Vocabulary

abbreviation a shortened form of a word; for example, *St.* for *Street,* *NJ* for *New Jersey*

application a form containing questions that ask for information about you, such as your name, address, and telephone number

catalog A college catalog is a book that describes a particular school, giving information on courses offered, how many points (credits) you receive for each course, when the school term begins and ends, and other information about the school.

closing a word or phrase used to end a letter. The closing is found just above the writer's signature and is always followed by a comma.

degree a title given by a school to a student who has finished the school's requirements satisfactorily. The degrees most commonly granted by U.S. four-year colleges are the Bachelor of Arts degree (B.A.) and the Bachelor of Science degree (B.S.).

fill out complete (an application or other form) by writing or typing into blank spaces all the information that is requested

indented form a format for writing letters in which the first line of each paragraph is placed farther in from the margin than the salutation

legible clear and easy to read

margin the space that is left empty on all four sides of a page containing a letter or other writing

modified block form a format for writing letters in which the margins are the same from the first line to the end. Nothing is indented. A blank space is left between paragraphs.

requirements those things that are necessary. For example, some colleges require incoming students to have taken four years of English and three years of science in high school; other colleges require at least two years of a language other than English. A college catalog will tell you the entrance requirements for that particular college.

return address the address of the person sending a note or letter

salutation the greeting in a letter, usually beginning with *Dear* followed by a person's name

signature a person's name written in his or her own handwriting

 **Example**

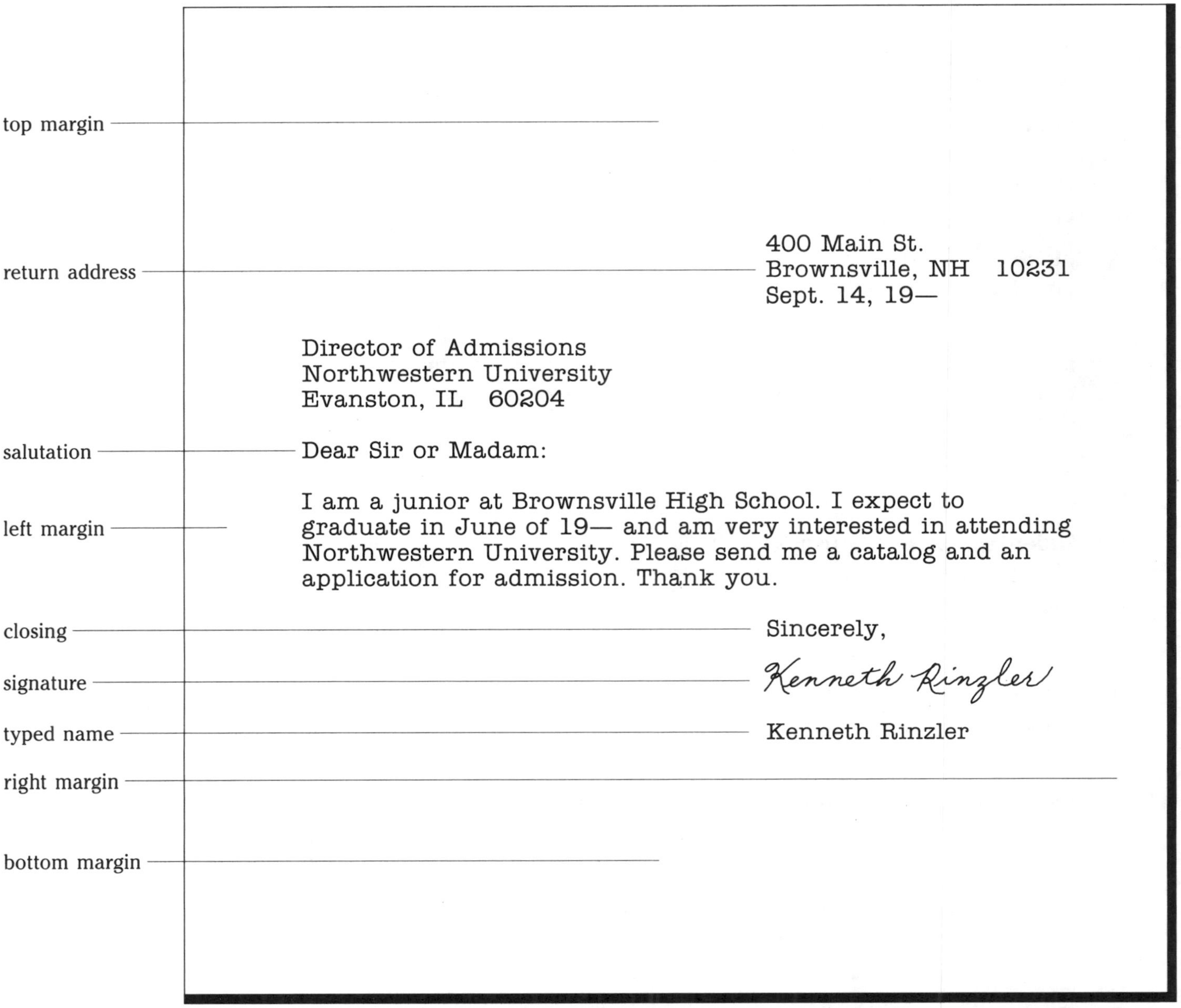

> 400 Main St.
> Brownsville, NH   10231
> Sept. 14, 19—
>
> Director of Admissions
> Northwestern University
> Evanston, IL   60204
>
> Dear Sir or Madam:
>
> I am a junior at Brownsville High School. I expect to
> graduate in June of 19— and am very interested in attending
> Northwestern University. Please send me a catalog and an
> application for admission. Thank you.
>
> > Sincerely,
> >
> > *Kenneth Rinzler*
> >
> > Kenneth Rinzler

Labels (pointing to the letter): top margin — return address — salutation — left margin — closing — signature — typed name — right margin — bottom margin

▶ Procedure A: Writing the Letter

1. Once you have decided where you think you would like to go to college, get the correct address for the school(s) of your choice. If possible, try to get the name of the director of admissions, to make your letter a little more personal. (Most school libraries and high school guidance departments have all kinds of books and catalogs containing information that will help you with this step.)

2. Use unlined stationery. If you have a typewriter or a word processor available, it's always nice to type your letter. Typed letters look more professional and are easier to read. If you are writing your letter by hand, be sure your writing is legible and neat.

3. Leave a margin on all sides of the stationery and center your letter so it looks good to the eye. If you are typing, use single spacing. Leave a blank space between

a. the return address and the address of the person you are writing to,

b. the address of the person you are writing to and the salutation,

c. the salutation and the body of the letter, and

d. the body of the letter and the closing.

4. Put your return address in the upper right-hand corner, with your number and street name on the first line; the city, state, and zip code on the second line; and the date on the third line. If you use one abbreviation in the address, use appropriate abbreviations throughout. In other words, if you write Main *St.* instead of Main *Street,* then write Brownsville, *NH* instead of Brownsville, *New Hampshire.* Either style is correct. Never write the date using all numerals, e.g., *9/14/90.* If you have used abbreviations in the address, abbreviate the month: *Sept.* 14, 1990. Otherwise, write out the name of the month.

Your return address is necessary so the director of admissions will know where to send the catalog and application you are requesting. You don't need to include your name here because that will appear at the bottom of your letter.

16 Maple St., Apt. 4F
Portland, OR 97223
Sept. 12, 19—

5. Leave a blank space below the date. Then, at the left side of the paper, write the name or title of the person you are writing to and his or her address. Follow the same rules for using abbreviations.

Ms. Maria Jiménez
Director of Admissions
University of Puerto Rico
Rio Piedras, PR 00924

6. Leave a blank space below the address. Then write *Dear* and the name of the person you are writing to. If you don't know the person's name or whether you're addressing a male or female, write *Dear Sir or Madam*. In business letters and other formal letters, the salutation is usually followed by a colon (:) instead of a comma.

```
                                        16 Maple St., Apt. 4F
                                        Portland, OR   97223
                                        Sept. 12, 19—

Ms. Maria Jiménez
Director of Admissions
University of Puerto Rico
Rio Piedras, PR   00924

Dear Ms. Jiménez:
```

7. Write your message. Be sure to tell the director of admissions what information you would like to receive about the school. Your message might look like one of these:

A. Indented Form

```
    I plan to graduate from high school in June 19— and
would like an application and catalog for the University of
Puerto Rico at Rio Piedras. Thank you.
```

B. Modified Block Form

I graduated from high school in May 19— and have been working as a data entry clerk since then. Now I would like to take some computer courses at the University of Puerto Rico at Rio Piedras. Please send me a catalog and application and any other information you think would be helpful. Thank you.

8. Under your message, on the right, end your letter with a word or phrase that shows your appreciation and interest. *Sincerely* is a good closing because it is not too formal and it says that you mean what you say. Sign your full name under the closing. If you type your letter, leave enough space to sign your name between the closing and your typed name.

Sincerely,

Alice Quon

Alice Quon

Your finished letter should look something like this:

16 Maple St., Apt. 4F
Portland, OR   97223
Sept. 12, 19—

Ms. Maria Jiménez
Director of Admissions
University of Puerto Rico
Rio Piedras, PR   00924

Dear Ms. Jiménez:

I plan to graduate from high school in June 19— and would
like an application and catalog for the University of Puerto
Rico at Rio Piedras. Thank you.

Sincerely,

Alice Quon

Alice Quon

▶ Practice A

Now it's your turn. Choose one of the two situations described below.

TASK: to write a letter requesting a college application

SITUATION 1: You are a junior in high school. You know there are essay questions on most college applications, and you want to know specifically what questions are asked by the college of your choice. You write a letter requesting a catalog and an application.

SITUATION 2: You are interested in taking courses at a community college (a local two-year college). You would like to know what courses are offered and would like to receive an application.

Remember the form:

_____

_____

_____

_____

_____

_____

_____

_____:

_____

_____

_____

_____

_____,

_____

▶ Procedure B: Addressing the Envelope

The name and address of the person/college you're writing to should be the same inside the letter and on the envelope. If you have typed your letter, the envelope should be typed, too.

1. Put your name and address (the *return address*) in the upper left-hand corner of the envelope so that if the letter cannot be delivered for some reason, it will be returned to you.

2. In the center of the envelope, write or type the name and address of the person you have written to. Put the person's name on one line, the name of the school on the next line, and the city, state, and zip code on the third line. If you know the street name and number, put that information on a separate line right after the name of the school. If the letter is going outside the country you are writing from, be sure

to put the name of the country on a line below the city, state, and zip code.

3. Put a postage stamp in the upper right-hand corner. Be sure to use the right amount of postage, or the letter will not be delivered.

Your finished envelope might look like this:

Ms. Alice Quon
16 Maple St., Apt. 4F
Portland OR   97223

Ms. Maria Jiménez, Director of Admissions
University of Puerto Rico
Rio Piedras, PR   00924

 Practice B
Now it's your turn.

TASK: to address the envelope

SITUATION: You have written a letter asking for a college application. Now you want to mail it.

▶ Procedure C: Folding the Letter

1. If you are using typing paper (8½″ by 11″), fold your paper in thirds. Start by folding the bottom edge up above the middle (a). Then fold the top down, over the bottom fold (b). Use a "business size" envelope.

a.

b.

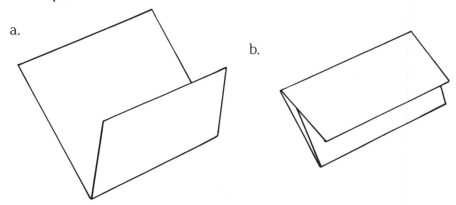

2. If you have written your letter on smaller stationery, use a matching envelope (one that is the appropriate size for the stationery). Smaller stationery is usually folded in half:

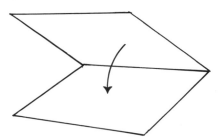

▶ Practice C

Now it's your turn.

TASK: to fold your letter properly

SITUATION: You have proofread your letter, checking your spelling, punctuation, names, and addresses. Your envelope is addressed. Fold your letter and put it in the envelope.

CHAPTER 6
Writing a Cover Letter for a Résumé

A résumé is a form of autobiography. It describes your work experience, educational background, and anything special about you that might help you get the kind of job you want. See "Writing a Résumé," pages 104–111, for more information about résumés.

Whenever you send a copy of your résumé to a prospective employer, you should send a letter along with it. This *cover letter* should be brief and specific. It should tell why you are sending your résumé and request the opportunity to be interviewed for a position.

Rationale
If you're interested in a specific job at a specific company, you'll want to send your résumé to that company. Unless you include a letter telling *why* you are sending the résumé, it may never be directed to the proper person or given any attention.

Materials Needed
typewriter or word processor, unlined paper, practice paper, name(s) and address(es) of prospective employers, envelope, postage stamp

Skills Involved
using correct letter-writing form; using correct spelling, capitalization, and punctuation; typing or word processing neatly; organizing thoughts

Important Vocabulary
at your convenience at a time that is good for you

autobiography a history of a person's life written by that person

body the main part of a letter; the message

closing a word or phrase used to end a letter. The closing is found just above the writer's signature and is always followed by a comma.

cover letter a letter sent with a person's résumé to a prospective employer, telling why that person is sending the résumé

indented form a format for writing letters in which the first line of each paragraph is placed farther in from the margin than the salutation. (See page 51 for an example.)

interview a meeting between two or more people. One person is usually at the interview for the purpose of applying for a job or for college. The other person or people are there to ask questions and to decide if the person being interviewed is right for the job or the college.

look forward to wait for with pleasure

modified block form a format for writing letters in which the margins are the same from the first line to the end. Nothing is indented. A blank space is left between paragraphs. (See page 39 for an example.)

résumé a list of a person's work and educational experience plus other important information about his or her background

return address the address of the person sending a note or letter

salutation the greeting in a letter, usually beginning with *Dear* followed by a person's name

```
                              400 Lane Drive
                              Albany, New York   12234
                              May 28, 19—

Dr. Susan Jones
New York State Education Department
Bureau of Bilingual Education
Albany, New York   12234

Dear Dr. Jones:

Enclosed is my résumé. I am applying for the position of
bilingual aide, Spanish/English, as advertised in The Daily
Chronicle, May 25, 19—.

I am available for an interview at your convenience and can
be reached at 518-555-0202. I look forward to hearing from
you.

                              Sincerely,

                              Olga Ortiz

                              Olga Ortiz
```

Procedure A: Writing the Letter

1. Use unlined paper and make a practice copy first so that your final letter will look professional. Remember, the first impression the reader gets of you will be a visual one.

a. Type your letter, using single spacing.

b. Be sure your letter is centered on the page. (It should *not* be all typed on the top half of the page with a lot of blank white space on the bottom half.)

By making a practice copy first, you can

a. correct any spelling, punctuation, or capitalization errors;

b. rewrite your sentences to make them as specific as they can be;

c. check to see that you have correctly followed either modified block or indented form; and

d. space your letter so that it is pleasing to the eye.

2. In the upper right corner of the paper, type your address (the *return address*) and the date.

```
                                    400 Lane Drive
                                    Albany, New York   12234
                                    May 28, 19—
```

3. Leave a blank space below the date. Then type the name and address of the person you are writing to on the left side of the paper. This person's name and address should be typed exactly as they will appear on the envelope.

```
Dr. Susan Jones
New York State Education Department
Bureau of Bilingual Education
Albany, New York   12234
```

4. Leave a blank space and then type the salutation.

```
Dear Dr. Jones:
```

5. Leave another blank space and then type the body of your letter. You can use either modified block form or indented form; just don't use a combination of both in the same letter. If you use modified block form, remember to leave a blank space between paragraphs to

show where each new paragraph begins. Your message might look like this:

> Enclosed is my résumé. I am applying for the position of bilingual aide, Spanish/English, as advertised in <u>The Daily Chronicle</u>, May 25, 19—.
>
> I am available for an interview at your convenience and can be reached at 518–555–0202. I look forward to hearing from you.

6. Leave a blank space and then finish your letter by typing *Sincerely* or another appropriate closing on the right. Leave enough space between the closing and your typed name to sign your name in ink.

Sincerely,

Olga Ortiz

Olga Ortiz

7. Read your letter again and correct any errors you find.

8. Sign your name in ink between the closing and your typed name, as shown above.

 ## Practice A
Now it's your turn.

TASK: to write a cover letter for your résumé

SITUATION: You have seen the job you've been waiting for advertised in the local newspaper. You want to send the company your résumé, and you need to write a cover letter to send with it.

The form will look something like this:

_____

_____

_____

_____

_____

_____

_____:

_____

_____

_____

_____

_____

_____,

_____

If the advertisement does not give the name of a specific person to write to, you can use *To whom it may concern* or *Dear Sir or Madam* as your salutation. The letter will then be given to the person responsible for reading it.

▶ Procedure B: Addressing the Envelope

The name and address of the person you're writing to should be typed the same way inside the letter and on the envelope.

1. Put your name and address (the *return address*) in the upper left corner of the envelope so that if the letter cannot be delivered for some reason, it will be returned to you.

2. In the center of the envelope, type the name and address of the person you have written to. Put his or her name on the first line. If you don't have a specific name, the first line should look exactly as it does in your letter. Next, type the name of the company or organization and its street name and number (if you have this information). The last line of the address should include the city, state, and zip code. If the letter is going outside the country you are writing from, add the name of the country you are sending the letter to and any other necessary information. All the information you need will be given in the advertisement you are answering.

3. Put a postage stamp in the upper right corner. Be sure to use the right amount of postage, or the letter will not be delivered.

Your finished envelope might look like this:

Ms. Olga Ortiz
400 Lane Dr.
Albany, NY   12234

Dr. Susan Jones
New York State Education Department
Bureau of Bilingual Education
Albany, NY   12234

Practice B

Now it's your turn.

TASK: to address the envelope

SITUATION: You have written a cover letter for your résumé. Now you want to mail them.

 Procedure C: Folding the Letter

See page 36 for instructions and diagrams describing the proper way to fold a letter before placing it in an envelope.

 Practice C

Now it's your turn.

TASK: to fold your letter properly

SITUATION: You have proofread your letter, checking your spelling, punctuation, names, and addresses. Your envelope is addressed. Fold your letter and put it in the envelope.

CHAPTER 7
Requesting an Interview

Whether you're applying for college or applying for a job, after you fill out the necessary applications, you may be asked to come in for an interview. This is a meeting between you and a college admissions director or you and someone who is interested in hiring you for a job. Even if you aren't asked to come in for an interview, it's a good idea to request one yourself. An interview gives you the chance to demonstrate why you would be a good student or employee. Also, the person who interviews you will remember you better than if he or she had just read your cover letter and résumé.

 Rationale

It is often easy and convenient to make an appointment for an interview by telephone. However, if you are applying for a job outside of your local area, or if you are requesting interviews at several different colleges, it makes more sense economically to write a short letter.

Another advantage to putting your request in writing is that you will have a better chance of reaching the person who is responsible for arranging an interview. That person may not be the one who answers the telephone if you call, and the message you leave may not be delivered correctly, or—worse yet—may never get delivered at all. When you put your request in writing, the appropriate person will have all the important information in front of him or her and can either write or call you to set the time and date for your interview.

Materials Needed

unlined typing paper or stationery; pen, typewriter or word processor; envelope; postage stamp

▷▷ Skills Involved

organizing thoughts; giving specific information; using correct spelling, punctuation, abbreviations, and capitalization

▷▷ Important Vocabulary

application a form containing questions that ask for information about you, such as your name, address, and telephone number

apply ask for; request

appointment a time and place arranged for people to meet

body the main part of a letter; the message

closing a word or phrase used to end a letter. The closing is found just above the writer's signature and is always followed by a comma.

hire give a job to

indented form a format for writing letters in which the first line of each paragraph is placed farther in from the margin than the salutation

interview a meeting between two or more people. One person is usually at the interview for the purpose of applying for a job or for college. The other person or people are there to ask questions and to decide if the person being interviewed is right for the job or the college.

legible clear and easy to read

modified block form a format for writing letters in which the margins are the same from the first line to the end. Nothing is indented. A blank space is left between paragraphs.

responsible for in charge of

return address the address of the person sending a note or letter

salutation the greeting in a letter, usually beginning with *Dear* followed by a person's name

signature a person's name written in his or her own handwriting

 **Example**

top margin	
return address	590 Park Ave. Middle Village, NY 11379 Nov. 23, 19—

Director of Admissions
Boston University
Boston, MA   02215

salutation — Dear Sir or Madam,

left margin —

I expect to graduate from Middle Village High School in June of 19—. I would like to attend Boston University and would appreciate an interview with you. I will be in Boston the week of December 22–29 and wonder if you could see me sometime during that week. If not, I would appreciate an appointment at a time that is convenient for you. Because I'm still in school, I would appreciate a date at the beginning or end of a week, if possible. Thank you.

closing — Sincerely,

signature — *Beth Malovic*

typed name — Beth Malovic

bottom margin —

right margin —

For an example of a cover letter requesting a job interview, see page 39.

▶ Procedure A: Writing the Letter

1. Use unlined stationery. If you have a typewriter or word processor available, it's always nice to type your letter. Typed letters look more professional and are easier to read. If you are writing your letter by hand, be sure your handwriting is legible and neat.

2. Leave a margin on all four sides of the paper and center your letter

so it looks good to the eye. If you are typing, use single spacing. Leave a blank space between

a. the return address and the address of the person you are writing to,

b. the address of the person you are writing to and the salutation,

c. the salutation and the body of the letter, and

d. the body of the letter and the closing.

3. Put your return address in the upper right-hand corner, with your street name and number on the first line; the city, state, and zip code on the second line; and the date on the third line. If you use one abbreviation in the address, use appropriate abbreviations throughout. In other words, if you write Park *Ave.* instead of Park *Avenue,* then write Middle Village, *NY* instead of Middle Village, *New York.* Either style is correct. If you use abbreviations in the address, abbreviate the month when you write the date: *Nov.* 23, 19—. Your return address is necessary so the person who receives your letter will know where to send a response. You don't need to include your name here because it will appear at the bottom of your letter.

590 Park Ave.
Middle Village, NY 11379
Nov. 23, 19—

4. Leave a blank space below the date. Then, on the left side of the paper, write the name or title of the person you are writing to and his or her address, following the same rules for abbreviations.

Director of Admissions
Boston University
Boston, MA 02215

5. Leave a blank space below the address. Then write *Dear* and the name of the person you are writing to on the left. If you don't know the person's name or whether you're addressing a male or female,

write *Dear Sir or Madam*. Put a colon or a comma after the salutation.

> 590 Park Ave.
> Middle Village, NY   11379
> Nov. 23, 19—
>
> Director of Admissions
> Boston University
> Boston, MA   02215
>
> Dear Sir or Madam,

6. Ask for an appointment for an interview. If you are going to be in the area of the college or company at a particular time, or if you are only available for an interview at certain times, state that information clearly in your letter. Look at these examples.

A. Indented Form

> I would appreciate an appointment for an interview during the Christmas vacation (December 22, 19— to January 3, 19—) or during our winter break, February 22–28, 19—, if possible.

B. Modified Block Form

> I will be graduating from Middle Village High School in June 19— and would like to attend Boston University. I am available for an interview at your convenience. I would appreciate it if the interview could be on a Saturday or at the beginning or end of a week so I don't miss too much school. Thank you.

7. Leave a blank space under your message. Then, on the right, end your letter with a word that shows your appreciation and interest. *Sincerely* is a good word because it is not too formal and it says that you mean what you say. Sign your full name under the closing. If you

type your letter, be sure to leave enough space for your signature between the closing and your typed name.

Sincerely,

Beth Malovic

Beth Malovic

Your finished letter should look something like this:

590 Park Ave.
Middle Village, NY   11379
Nov. 23, 19—

Director of Admissions
Boston University
Boston, MA   02215

Dear Sir or Madam,

I will be graduating from Middle Village High School in June 19— and would like to attend Boston University. I am available for an interview at your convenience. I would appreciate it if the interview could be on a Saturday or at the beginning or end of a week so I don't miss too much school. Thank you.

Sincerely,

Beth Malovic

Beth Malovic

Now it's your turn.

TASK: to write a letter requesting an appointment for an interview

SITUATION: You are a senior in high school. You would like to visit several colleges and have interviews with their directors of admissions. You are going to be in Providence, Rhode Island, during the week of February 12–19 and would like an interview at Brown University. The zip code for the school is 02906.

Remember the form:

_____

_____

_____

_____

_____

_____

_____:

_____

_____

_____

_____

_____,

_____

Procedure B: Addressing the Envelope

The name and address of the person you're writing to should be written or typed the same way inside the letter and on the envelope.

1. Put your name and address (the *return address*) in the upper left-hand corner of the envelope so that if the letter cannot be delivered for some reason, it will be returned to you.

2. In the center of the envelope, write or type the name and address of the person you have written to. Put the person's name or title on the first line, the name of the college on the next line, and the city, state, and zip code on a third line. If you know the street name and number, put that information on a separate line just above the city, state, and zip code. If the letter is going outside the country you are writing from, be sure to put the name of the country on a fourth line.

3. Put a postage stamp in the upper right-hand corner. Be sure to use the right amount of postage, or the letter will not be delivered.

Your finished envelope should look something like this:

```
Ms. Beth Malovic
590 Park Ave.
Middle Village, NY   11379




                    Director of Admissions
                    Boston University
                    Boston, MA   02215
```

Practice B

Now it's your turn.

TASK: to address the envelope

SITUATION: You have written a letter requesting an interview. Now you want to mail it.

 Procedure C: Folding the Letter

See page 36 for instructions and diagrams describing the proper way to fold a letter before placing it in an envelope.

 Practice C

Now it's your turn.

TASK: to fold your letter properly

SITUATION: You have proofread your letter, checking your spelling, punctuation, names, and addresses. Your envelope is addressed. Fold your letter and put it in the envelope.

CHAPTER 8
Writing a Letter of Complaint

In this age of computers and machines, it's very hard to find a person to talk to when you find an error on a bill or on an order for merchandise bought through the mail. In most companies, everything seems to be handled by machines: everything, that is, except correcting errors.

▷▷ Rationale

If you find a mistake on a bill, you can call the company and try to have it corrected, but there can be many problems with this approach, such as

1. you have nothing in writing to prove that you have notified the company of the error;

2. the person you speak to may not be qualified to correct the error or may forget to take care of it and later deny any knowledge of it;

3. you may end up having to pay interest on the unpaid bill until the error is corrected and, worse, you may spoil your good credit rating.

If you write a letter of complaint and keep a copy of it, you have proof that you have notified the company about the error. In the letter, you can explain exactly what is wrong so that (a) the problem will be directed to the right person, and (b) all the information is there in writing for the person to check so he or she doesn't have to try to remember what you said. If you have any receipts, you can send *copies* of them along to prove your points. (You'll want to save the original bills and receipts for yourself.)

▷▷ Materials Needed

practice paper, unlined stationery, envelope, pen (or typewriter), bill, receipts, correct mailing address, access to a copying machine or carbon paper, postage stamp

Skills Involved

using correct spelling, punctuation, and capitalization; using correct letter form; supplying specific details in organized paragraphs

Important Vocabulary

bill a piece of paper that tells how much money you owe someone for merchandise you bought or for services (such as the telephone or electricity) you used

closing a word or phrase used to end a letter. The closing is found just above the writer's signature and is always followed by a comma.

complaint an expression of unhappiness or dissatisfaction about something

credit rating If you charge items to credit cards and fail to pay your bills, you will get a bad credit rating. This information is available to other companies and might make it difficult for you to charge things or obtain loans in the future.

enclosed inside. If you have enclosed something in a letter, it means you have put it in the envelope with the letter. The abbreviation *Enc* at the end of a business letter tells the reader to look for other items in the envelope.

merchandise items for sale

notified informed

Re about; with regard to. Often used at the beginning of a business letter to indicate the subject of the letter.

receipt a written statement showing that you have received certain merchandise or have paid a certain amount of money

return address the address of the person sending a note or letter

salutation the greeting in a letter, usually beginning with *Dear* followed by a person's name

shipping and handling charges When you order merchandise through the mail, you often are charged for the cost of shipping (mailing) and handling (assembling and preparing for mailing) your order.

To whom it may concern a salutation used when you don't know the name or title of the person you should write to

157 Ridge Ave.
Seattle, WA 98110
April 14, 19—

Rick Rabbit Emporium
P.O. Box 5555
Portland, OR 97223

Re: Order # 85942

To whom it may concern:

On March 1, I ordered <u>3</u> pink rabbits at $9.95 each and <u>3</u> flower baskets at $11.95 each for a total of $65.70 plus shipping and handling, $11.50. This brings the final total to $77.20.

Enclosed is a copy of your receipt, which came with my order. Today I received a bill for $87.15 for <u>4</u> pink rabbits and 3 flower baskets. Since I didn't order <u>4</u> rabbits and I never received <u>4</u> rabbits, I'm enclosing a check for the original amount, $77.20, for the merchandise I did receive. Please correct your billing. Thank you.

Sincerely,

Prunella Pasquale

Enc

problem is stated here

▶ Procedure A: Writing the Letter

1. Write a practice copy first so you can proofread it and correct any mistakes or add anything you may have left out the first time.

2. On unlined stationery, put your return address and the date in the upper right corner. This information is extremely important for easy identification and so an answer can be mailed to you.

157 Ridge Ave.
Seattle, WA 98110
April 14, 19

3. Leave a blank space below the date. Then, on the left, write the name and address of the company that sent you the incorrect bill.

Rick Rabbit Emporium
P.O. Box 5555
Portland, OR 97223

4. If you have an account number or any kind of order number, leave a blank space and write it below the company's address. This information makes it easier for the person who receives your letter to check into the problem.

Re: Order # 85942

5. Leave a blank space and then write the salutation. If you don't know the name or title of a particular person to write to, write:

To whom it may concern :

This will get your letter directed to the right person.

6. Leave a blank space below the salutation and write your message. Be very specific. Tell exactly what the problem is. If you have been

charged for merchandise you never ordered or for merchandise you ordered but never received, say so, telling exactly what merchandise you're talking about and giving the price.

If you have been charged an incorrect amount, tell what the correct amount should be and enclose *copies* of any receipts or proof you might have. Don't send originals unless you make copies of them for yourself. These documents are all the proof you have.

7. Leave a blank space below your message and put your closing on the right. *Sincerely* is a good word to use for the closing. Sign your complete name under your closing. If you type your letter, leave enough space between the closing and your typed name to sign your name in ink.

Sincerely,

Prunella Pasquale

Prunella Pasquale

8. Below your name, on the left, put *Enc* to indicate that you have enclosed other items in the envelope.

9. Make a copy of your letter to keep for yourself. At the same time, make copies of the bill and any receipts you want to send with the letter.

 ## Practice A

Now it's your turn.

TASK: to write a letter of complaint

SITUATION: You have received a bill from ABC Shirt and Pants Mail Order, P.O. Box 2143, Garden City, NY 11535, for two shirts and two pairs of pants you ordered through the mail. You ordered two shirts, size medium, on sale at $17.95 a shirt and two pairs of pants, size large, at $27.50 a pair. Shipping and handling charges were $9.95. You were billed for two shirts at the regular price of $20.95. The other charges were correct. Your order number was 1432648. Write a letter to the company explaining the problem.

Read your letter over again and ask yourself these questions:

1. Did you tell exactly what you ordered and how much each item cost?

2. Did you remember to add up the amount you should have been charged?

▶ Procedure B: Addressing the Envelope

The name and address of the company you're writing to should be written or typed the same way inside the letter and on the envelope.

1. Put your name and address (the *return address)* in the upper left-hand corner of the envelope so that if the letter cannot be delivered for some reason, it will be returned to you.

2. In the center of the envelope, write or type the name and address of the company you have written to. Put the name of the company on the first line, the street name and number (or P.O. box number) on the next line, and the city, state, and zip code on a third line. If the letter is going outside the country you are writing from, be sure to put the name of the country on a fourth line.

3. Put a postage stamp in the upper right-hand corner. Be sure to use the right amount of postage, or the letter will not be delivered.

Your finished envelope should look something like this:

Prunella Pasquale
157 Ridge Ave.
Seattle, WA 98110

Rick Rabbit Emporium
P. O. Box 5555
Portland, OR 97223

Practice B

Now it's your turn.

TASK: to address the envelope

SITUATION: You have written a letter of complaint. Now you want to mail it.

CHAPTER 9
Ordering Tickets Through the Mail

You're planning a vacation in New York next month. While you're there, you would like to see a Broadway show or a ballet at Lincoln Center. Since you know when you'd like to go to the theater and how much money you want to spend, writing a letter with a check or money order enclosed is a good way to get the tickets of your choice.

 Rationale

There are many ways to get tickets for a show, concert, sporting event, or other performance. You can (1) call on the telephone and give a credit card number, (2) go to the theater or arena where the event will take place, or (3) write for tickets.

If you call on the telephone, you have the advantage of knowing immediately if and when tickets are available. The disadvantages are that (1) you don't always know where your seats will be, (2) you must have a credit card to pay for the tickets, and (3) you must pay a service charge for each ticket. If you live near the theater or arena, you can go right to the box office to buy your tickets. The advantages to this are that you will know immediately what seats are available on what dates. You also have the choice of paying by cash, credit card, or check. The disadvantages to this method are that (1) the box office may not be open when you are free to go there, and (2) you may not live or work in the area.

The third alternative is to write a letter of request. The only disadvantage to this approach is that you have to wait to hear if the seats you want are available at the times you requested. Naturally, the more time you give the theater to fill your request, the better chance you have of receiving the tickets you want.

Materials Needed

unlined stationery or typing paper, two envelopes, pen or typewriter, check or money order, postage stamps

Skills Involved

writing a check or purchasing a money order; organizing thoughts; giving specific details; using correct spelling, punctuation, and capitalization

Important Vocabulary

arena an area used for sports or other entertainment, usually enclosed in a building

balcony an upper level containing seats in a theater

box office a place where you can buy tickets for the theater or other events

closing a word or phrase used to end a letter. The closing is found just above the writer's signature and is always followed by a comma.

concert a performance or show given by one or more musicians

Enc abbreviation for *enclosure;* written at the end of a letter when you have included items other than the letter in the envelope

matinee an afternoon performance

mezzanine the lowest balcony in a theater (or, sometimes, the first few rows of seats in the lowest balcony)

money order a kind of check purchased from a bank or post office for a specific amount of money; often used for sending a payment through the mail

return address the address of the person sending a note or letter

self-addressed, stamped envelope an envelope addressed to you with the correct postage on it. You enclose this envelope with your letter of request so the tickets you ask for can be mailed to you as quickly as possible. You will often see this abbreviated as SASE.

service charge here, an extra charge that is added to the price of tickets when you order them by telephone

103 Smith St.
Minneapolis, MN 55403
Nov. 24, 19—

Box Office
New York City Ballet
New York State Theater
Lincoln Center
New York, NY 10023

Enclosed are a self-addressed, stamped envelope and a check for eighty dollars ($80.00). Please send me two (2) tickets for the best possible seats, center mezzanine, for The Nutcracker ballet for Monday evening, December 25; Tuesday evening, December 26; or Wednesday matinee, December 27. Location is important, but I will be in New York for those dates only, so I would appreciate the best possible seats you can give me for one of those three dates. Thank you.

Sincerely,

Phutak Chong

Phutak Chong

Enc

Procedure A: Writing the Letter

1. Use unlined paper and be sure to write clearly in ink (or use a typewriter or word processor). You can use small stationery as long as there is enough room in the envelope for the letter, a check or money order, and a return envelope.

2. Put your return address and the date in the upper right-hand corner.

> 14 Beverly Dr.
> Los Angeles, CA   90024
> June 1, 19—

3. Leave a blank space below the date. Then, on the left side of the paper, write the address as it will appear on the envelope.

Phantom of the Opera
P.O. Box 993
Times Square Station
New York, NY   10108

4. Leave a blank space and then write your message. Explain what you are including in the envelope and describe the specific tickets you want. Be sure to tell (a) the date or dates you want the tickets for, (b) the number of tickets you want, and (c) where you would prefer to sit. If you give more than one date, you might want to tell which is your first choice. If you give only one specific date, ask for "the best possible seats" rather than specifying a particular location, especially if the play, ballet, or concert is very popular. At the end of your message, it's always nice to say "thank you."

Enclosed are a self-addressed, stamped envelope and a money order for sixty dollars ($60.00). Please send two (2) tickets, center mezzanine, for Wednesday, July 5, for Phantom of the Opera. Since that is the only time I will be in New York, I would appreciate the best seats possible for that date. Thank you.

5. Leave a blank space, then put your closing on the right side of the paper and sign your complete name under it. If you are typing your letter, leave enough space between the closing and your typed name to sign your name in ink.

6. Below your name, on the left, put *Enc* to indicate that you have enclosed other items in the envelope. See the example at the top of the next page.

Sincerely,

Ludmila Tcheroff

Ludmila Tcheroff

Enc

7. Address an envelope to yourself and put on the correct postage.

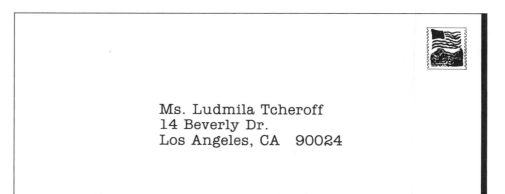

Ms. Ludmila Tcheroff
14 Beverly Dr.
Los Angeles, CA   90024

8. If you are enclosing a check, make it out to the name of the show. On the bottom of the check, write what it is for so that if it should get separated from your letter, it will be easy to identify. A money order should have the same information written on it.

9. Put the check inside your letter and put them in an envelope with the self-addressed envelope. Be sure all the items are enclosed.

 Practice A

Now it's your turn.

TASK: to order tickets for a concert

SITUATION: Your favorite musical group is coming to a theater in a city near you next month. They will be performing there for one week. You want to order tickets for you and a friend for a Saturday evening or Sunday matinee performance. Be sure to enclose a self-addressed, stamped envelope and a check or money order.

Procedure B: Addressing the Envelope

1. Put your name and address (the *return address*) in the upper left-hand corner of the envelope so that if the letter cannot be delivered for some reason, it will be returned to you.

2. In the center of the envelope, write or type the address of the theater or box office exactly as it appears on your letter.

3. Put a postage stamp in the upper right-hand corner. Be sure to use the right amount of postage, or the letter will not be delivered.

Your finished envelope should look something like this:

Ms. Ludmila Tcheroff
14 Beverly Drive
Los Angeles, CA   90024

Phantom of the Opera
P.O. Box 993
Times Square Station
New York, NY   10108

Practice B

Now it's your turn.

TASK: to address the envelope

SITUATION: You have written a letter requesting tickets to a concert.
Now you want to mail it.

Hope you get good seats!

UNIT
THREE

APPLICATIONS AND RÉSUMÉS

CHAPTER 10
Filling Out a College Application

Filling out a college application is an experience you won't soon forget. To do it properly requires time and patience. However, it isn't difficult if you follow the directions and practice on a "dummy" or blank piece of paper first. Rule Number One in filling out a college application is DON'T . . . don't fill it out until you follow the steps shown under **Procedure** in this chapter.

 ## Rationale

The rationale for filling out a college application is easy: if you want to go to college, you must follow the necessary procedures. One of the first steps you must take is to send for and fill out an application from the school(s) of your choice. (See "Requesting a College Application," pages 26–36.)

 ## Materials Needed

pencils, pen, typewriter or word processor if application must be typed, scrap paper, application, envelope, appropriate postage, information required by college (for example, parents' financial aid statement), check or money order for any application fee(s)

 ## Skills Involved

reading comprehension; paying attention to details, spelling, grammar, and punctuation; outlining; selecting and organizing appropriate material for writing a coherent essay; essay writing; using neat, legible handwriting; typing (if required); meeting deadlines; following directions

Important Vocabulary

Admission Committee the group of people who read your application and decide if you should be admitted to a school

application fee money that must be sent (by check or money order, never cash) with your application for admission to some colleges

assets things that have monetary value, such as a house, a car, or a savings account

brochure a small printed booklet

campus the grounds and buildings of a college or university

candidate someone who is applying for a certain position

class rank a number assigned to a student to indicate his or her position among all the students at that grade level. Class rank is determined by comparing each student's course grades to the grades of the other class members.

credentials written proof of your abilities, qualifications, suitability for a position

deposit here, an amount of money that must be sent to a school (once you have been accepted) to indicate that you do plan to attend that school. The deposit holds your place in the school and is usually *nonrefundable,* which means you will not get the money back if you decide later not to go to that school.

dormitory a college-owned building with living quarters for students. Dormitories usually contain bedrooms, bathrooms, communal living rooms, and sometimes a dining area.

essay here, a relatively short piece of writing that expresses the writer's feelings or opinions on a certain subject

family income the amount of money your family earns in a year

fee waiver a decision to allow someone not to pay a normally required fee (amount of money)

financial aid money (usually in the form of loans, scholarships, and/or paid jobs on campus) provided to a student to help pay for his or her college education

forfeit lose; give up

foster parents persons (not biological parents) who are in charge of a child's financial support and well-being

freshman a first-year student in high school or college

funds money

guardian a person who is legally responsible for the well-being of another person

interview a meeting between an applicant for a school or job and the person(s) who will decide if the applicant is right for the school or job. See "Requesting an Interview," pages 46–55.

outline here, an organized list of the main ideas to be expressed in an essay

proofread read for the purpose of finding or correcting any errors

reservation a guarantee that a place has been saved for someone

scrap paper extra paper; paper that is not intended for a specific purpose

submit send in or present

transcript a record of a student's marks or grades at a particular school

transfer student a student who has attended one school and changes to another school before completing the requirements for a degree

waiting list here, a list of people who are in line to be accepted by a school. If a place at the school becomes available, the next person on the waiting list will be accepted.

 Example
See next page.

Application for Admission
and Financial Aid

NORTHWESTERN

Instructions

1

Applying to Northwestern

When you apply for admission to Northwestern, you may choose the Early Plan or the Regular Plan. Because candidates accepted on the Early Plan must reply by March 1, you should choose the Early Plan only if the other colleges to which you are applying will notify you well before March 1. If your clear preference is Northwestern University, the Early Plan will ensure a decision before many application deadlines for other colleges. Early Plan candidates are either offered or refused admission; there is no waiting list.

Deadlines	Early Plan	Regular Plan
Application for Admission	November 1: Parts I and II	January 1: Parts I and II
Admission Decision	December 15	April 15
Candidates' Reply	March 1	May 1
Room Reservation	Before April 1	Before June 1

Application Fee

Submit the required $35 application fee with Part I of the Application for Admission. If your family income is less than $12,000 a year and your family has limited assets, you may request a fee waiver. A letter stating these conditions and signed by you and your parents should accompany Part I. Without such a letter or the application fee, your application will not be reviewed by the Admission Committee.

Early Plan

Financial Aid Candidates
See instruction 2. You will use the Special Early Version Financial Aid Form, which we will send to you when we receive Part I.

Deposit Deadlines
To accept the offer of admission, you must submit a nonrefundable tuition deposit/prepayment of $200 by March 1. You must also send a nonrefundable room reservation deposit/prepayment of $200 before April 1. Both deposits must be received by the deadlines, or you will forfeit the offer of admission.

Reply Deadline Change
To change the reply date from March 1 to May 1, you must request the change before the Admission Office has mailed a decision. If a decision on an application for admission has been mailed, the reply deadline will not be changed. You will be considered under the Regular Plan if you have been granted a reply deadline change.

Regular Plan

Financial Aid Candidates
If you are applying for financial aid, see instruction 2.

Deposit Deadlines
To accept the offer of admission, you must submit a nonrefundable tuition deposit/prepayment of $200 by May 1. You must also send a nonrefundable room reservation deposit/prepayment of $200 before June 1. Both deposits must be received by the deadlines, or you will forfeit the offer of admission.

Foreign Students
In addition to the credentials required of all applicants to Northwestern University, foreign students should present the results of the Test of English as a Foreign Language (TOEFL). They should request the special brochure "Information for Foreign Students."

2

Financial Aid

When to Apply

Do not wait until you have been admitted to Northwestern to apply for financial aid. If you fail to meet your deadline for filing the Financial Aid Form (FAF), notification of financial aid will be delayed, and funds for financial aid may be entirely committed. Prompt filing ensures that you will receive an aid decision with your admission decision or shortly thereafter. We cannot give you an extension of your reply deadline if you file late.

	Early Plan	Regular Plan
FAF Filing Deadline	November 15	February 15

You must file the FAF with the College Scholarship Service (CSS) no later than the filing deadline. To ensure timely processing, we recommend that you file the FAF at the same time that you submit the Application for Admission.

How to Apply

Freshman Candidates
■ Check "yes" for question 15, Part I (page 1) of the Application for Admission. Complete the Request for Financial Aid Consideration after discussion with your parents. You must request consideration to receive a financial aid decision.
■ Complete the FAF, including side 2, and send it to the CSS by your filing deadline. You must list Northwestern University (code number 1565) as a recipient of the FAF.
■ Use estimated income tax figures for 1987 if tax returns are not completed. Financial aid awards will be adjusted later if the actual income differs significantly from the estimated income.

Early Plan: Use the Special Early Version FAF, available only from the Office of Admission. We will send it to you on receipt of Part I, or we will send one earlier if you request it.

Regular Plan: Use the regular FAF, available from secondary schools in the fall.

Transfer Students
Complete the Northwestern Transfer Student Financial Aid Application and a Financial Aid Transcript, both available from the Office of Admission. You must also submit a regular FAF to CSS *at least one month before the application deadline for the quarter you wish to enter* (see instruction 4).

Illinois Residents

Apply for the Monetary Grant awarded by the Illinois State Scholarship Commission (ISSC) by submitting the FAF and checking the appropriate box on the FAF for the information to be sent to ISSC.

Foreign Nationals

Foreign nationals must be permanent residents of the United States to be eligible for financial aid from Northwestern. Those receiving financial aid will be asked to submit proof of permanent resident status if they enroll at Northwestern.

Divorced or Separated Parents

If your parents are separated or divorced, the custodial parent must complete the FAF. If they have been separated or divorced for less than three years or if the noncustodial parent claims you as a tax exemption, the noncustodial parent is *required* to complete the Divorced/Separated Parents Statement, available from the Office of Admission. Noncustodial parents falling outside these categories may also be required to submit the statement. *Financial aid will not be awarded to students whose parents fail to comply with these requirements.*

Business/Farm Owners

Owners of businesses and/or farms should complete the Business/Farm Supplement, available from secondary schools or the Office of Admission, when they complete the FAF. The supplement can be submitted to CSS with the FAF or forwarded directly to Northwestern.

Independent Students

To be an independent student at Northwestern, you must be at least 23 years old and must not have been taken as a tax exemption by, lived with, or received any support from your parents during the previous three years. The parents of independent students are not required to complete their portion of the FAF. Federal guidelines regarding independent student status differ from Northwestern's.

National Merit/National Achievement Scholarships

Northwestern is a sponsor of the National Merit and National Achievement scholarships. To be considered for either scholarship, you must apply to Northwestern and notify the National Merit Scholarship Corporation that Northwestern is your first choice. You also must file the FAF and demonstrate financial need.

NROTC/AFROTC/Army ROTC

NROTC/AFROTC/Army ROTC scholarships at Northwestern cover all or part of the cost of tuition plus a monthly stipend of $100. If you are an NROTC/AFROTC/Army ROTC candidate and cannot afford the full cost of a Northwestern education, you should also apply for financial aid, in case you do not receive a military scholarship.

Cost of a Northwestern Education

The average student budget for the academic year 1987-88 appears below. Financial aid awards are based on this budget and include a travel allowance for two round trips between your home and Chicago.

Tuition	$11,637
Room and Board	3,999
Books and Supplies	500
Personal Expenses	810
Total	$16,946

These amounts are subject to change; increases should be expected in subsequent years.

3

Academic Credentials

Secondary School Report

A transcript, your class rank, and a counselor's statement must be provided (see pages 9 and 10). If you apply on the Regular Plan, you must provide your senior-year grades (seventh semester or first term).

Tests

All tests should be taken before your application deadline.

Required Test

- Scholastic Aptitude Test (SAT) or
- American College Test (ACT)

Achievement Tests

Achievement Tests are strongly recommended but not required.

Recommended Achievement Tests

If you apply to...	Take...
College of Arts and Sciences, Schools of Education and Social Policy, Journalism, Speech	English plus two others (English Composition with essay acceptable but not required)
Technological Institute	English Mathematics (Level I or II) Chemistry or Physics
School of Music	Audition required (Achievement Tests optional)

Three Achievement Tests are required for the Honors Program in Medical Education (see page 7), the Integrated Science Program, and Mathematical Methods in the Social Sciences (see instruction 6).

Transfer and Returning Adult Students

Applying to Northwestern

Transfer and returning adult candidates may submit an application any time after the college year begins.

Enrollment Date	Application Deadline
Fall	June 1
Winter	November 1
Spring	February 1
Summer	May 1

Admission decisions for fall quarter candidates are made from mid-April through July.

(over)

Admission Procedures

Transfer Students

Transfer candidates should request the pamphlet "Information for Transfer Candidates." They must present at least one year of college work. No more than two years of credit will be awarded to admitted transfer students.

To complete a transfer application, please submit
- Application for Admission, Parts I and II
- All college and secondary school transcripts
- Dean's Reference Form
- Test Scores: SAT or ACT

School of Music candidates: an audition is required.

Interviews are strongly recommended but not required.

Returning Adult Students

Candidates who completed up to two years of college work more than five years ago should call or write the Office of Admission for the Returning Adult Student Application.

Financial Aid Candidates

If you are applying for financial aid, see instruction 2.

5

Interviews/Auditions

Interviews

Interviews are strongly recommended and may be held before you submit your application. Call (312) 491-4395 or write to the Office of Admission for an appointment. Because the number of interview appointments is limited, call or write at least three weeks before your requested interview date, or no later than a month before the interview deadline.

	Early Plan	Regular Plan
Interview Deadline	November 1	February 1

Overnight accommodations in University housing are available during October, November, January, and February. You should make your reservation to stay in a dormitory when you schedule your interview or at least three weeks before your proposed visit.

Off-Campus Interviews

Alumni conduct interviews in their home communities between October 1 and January 20 and prefer that you schedule your appointment before January 1. For more information about an off-campus interview, call (312) 491-7271 or write to the Office of Admission.

Auditions

Auditions are required for all candidates to the School of Music. For more information contact the Office of Admission or the School of Music, (312) 491-3141.

6

Special Programs for Freshmen

Honors Program in Medical Education

HPME candidates must complete the Request for Application that is on pages 7 and 8.

Integrated Science Program and Mathematical Methods in the Social Sciences

Candidates who are interested in applying to ISP or MMSS (see Part I, question 26) will be sent the required application by

Director	Director
Integrated Science Program	Mathematical Methods in
Northwestern University	the Social Sciences
Evanston, Illinois 60201	Northwestern University
	Evanston, Illinois 60201

Completed applications for either program should be returned by February 1 (Early and Regular Plan).

Achievement Tests

Tests must be taken by the December test date by all candidates for the Honors Program in Medical Education and by Early Plan candidates for the Integrated Science Program and Mathematical Methods in the Social Sciences. Regular Plan candidates for ISP and MMSS must take tests by the January test date. Required tests:

- **HPME**
English
Mathematics Level II
Chemistry (Physics acceptable but not preferred)
- **ISP**
English
Mathematics Level II
Chemistry or Physics
- **MMSS**
English
Any two others

7-87/8OM/AR-MH/3645

1

Northwestern University • Application for Admission   *Part I*

Apply as early as possible. You may return Part I now, before returning Part II, with the $35 application fee and the acknowledgment card. Put your name and Social Security number on the check. Use the enclosed envelope addressed to Office of Admission, Northwestern University, P.O. Box 3060 – 1801 Hinman Avenue, Evanston, Illinois 60204-3060.

Please print or type

1. **Freshman candidates** for fall quarter, indicate the Early Plan or the Regular Plan (see instructions 1 and 3)
   ☐ Early Plan   ☒ Regular Plan
   Deadline, November 1   Deadline, January 1

   Freshman candidates for other quarters, indicate the calendar year and quarter you wish to enter
   19_____ ☐ Winter (January)   ☐ Spring (March)   ☐ Summer (June)
            Deadline, November 1   Deadline, February 1   Deadline, May 1

2. **Transfer candidates**, indicate the calendar year and quarter you wish to enter (see instruction 4)
   19_____ ☐ Fall (September)   ☐ Winter (January)   ☐ Spring (March)   ☐ Summer (June)
            Deadline, June 1   Deadline, November 1   Deadline, February 1   Deadline, May 1

3. Have you previously applied for admission? ☐ Yes/year_____ ☒ No   Do you have a course catalog? ☐ Yes ☒ No

4. Check one   ☐ Male ☒ Female

5. Name in full   <u>Kohn</u>   <u>Tova</u>
         last (family)   first   middle
   Have you ever used another name? If so, what? ——

6. Permanent address <u>1410 Abbot St.   Lincolnwood   IL   60646</u> Telephone <u>555</u> <u>555-1279</u>
        number and street   city   state   zip   area code   number

7. Current mailing address <u>same as above</u>   Telephone
        number and street   city   state   zip   area code   number
   Current mailing address effective until what date? _____
             month   date   year

8. Social Security number   <u>123-45-6789</u>

9. Date of birth <u>12</u> <u>15</u> <u>72</u>   Place of birth <u>Tierra del Fuego</u>   <u>Cuba</u>
      month day year   city   state   county or province   country

10. Citizenship status   ☐ (1) U.S. citizen   ☒ (3) Permanent resident of U.S. but not a U.S. citizen
    ☐ (2) Nonresident alien (list visa type _____) Country, if not U.S., of which you are a citizen <u>Cuba</u>

11. Racial/ethnic information. Please check one. Furnishing or failing to furnish this optional information will not affect your admission decision.
    ☐ (1) American Indian/Alaskan native   ☐ (3) Asian American/Pacific islander   ☐ (2) Black/Negro, not   ☐ (8) Puerto Rican
                                                              of Hispanic origin
    ☐ (7) Mexican American/Chicano   ☐ (4) Hispanic, not Puerto Rican   ☐ (6) Caucasian/White,
                                   or Mexican American   not of Hispanic origin

12. Is a language other than English spoken at home?   ☒ Yes What language? <u>Spanish</u>   ☐ No

13. Are you a U.S. Armed Forces veteran?   ☐ Yes ☒ No

14. Where do you plan to live while attending Northwestern? ☐ University housing ☒ At home ☐ Off campus

15. Are you seeking financial aid from Northwestern?   ☒ Yes If yes, complete the "Request for Financial Aid Consideration" ☐ No

16. Do you plan to participate in intercollegiate debate?   ☐ Yes ☒ No

All candidates: Be sure to complete all questions (17-27) on the reverse side of this page.

Request for Financial Aid Consideration (see instruction 2)

Note: This section should be completed only by candidates who are requesting financial aid consideration. The families of such candidates must submit a copy of the Financial Aid Form to the College Scholarship Service.

a. Please indicate an estimate of the amount of money that will be provided for your freshman year from the following sources:

Parents <u>$4,500</u>   Your Contribution <u>$1,000</u>

b. Did your grandfather or great-grandfather serve
   in the American Armed Forces in World War I? ☐ Yes (Noyes Scholarship)   ☒ No

c. Are you of Serbian descent?   ☐ Yes (Duchich Scholarship)   ☒ No

d. Do you intend to apply for one of these
   scholarships?   ☐ NROTC ☐ AFROTC ☐ AROTC ☒ National Merit/National Achievement

e. What outside sources of assistance, e.g., corporate, civic, fraternal support, do you hope to qualify for? ——

(Over)

Northwestern University • Application for Admission *Part 1*

17. Father's name   Kohn   Abraham   Mother's name   Kohn   Ruth   Llano
                   last   first   initial   last   first   maiden

Address   1410   Abbot St.   Address   1410   Abbot St.
       number   street   number   street

     Lincolnwood   IL   60646   Lincolnwood   IL   60646
         city   state zip   city   state zip

Telephone   555   555-1279   Telephone   555   555-1279
       area code   number   area code   number

Employer   Whistler's Restaurant   Employer   Oak Brook Manufacturing Co.
if self-employed, indicate nature of business   if self-employed, indicate nature of business

Position   waiter   Position   factory worker

Place of birth   Havana, Cuba   Place of birth   Havana, Cuba

High school attended   Colegio Superior de Havana   4
              name   no. of years
High school attended   Colegio Superior de Havana   3

College(s) attended   Universidad Nacional   4
        name   no. of years
College(s) attended   —
        name   no. of years

Degrees   B.S.   If deceased, give date   —   Degrees   —   If deceased, give date   —

18. If you have foster parents or a guardian, please give names and address   —

19. Relatives who have attended Northwestern (indicate relationship, dates of attendance, and school attended)   —

20. Brothers or sisters: how many older?   2   did any attend college?   1   how many younger?   1

21. Secondary School   City/State   From (yr/mo) To   Graduation Date   School Type

Current   Lincolnwood High School   Lincolnwood, IL   9/86-6/90   June '90

☒ (1) Public
☐ (2) Parochial

Last Previous

☐ (3) Independent
☐ (4) Military

if more than two, attach a separate list

22. College Board/ACT code number of last high school attended   0001

23. Postsecondary education (including nursing, dental hygiene, and technical schools; if more than one, attach additional names on a separate sheet)

College Current or last attended	City/State	From (yr/mo) To	Number of Courses to Date	Degree/Year
—				

☐ full time   ☐ part time   ☐ summer only   ☐ not for credit   ☐ high school credit

24. School or program to which you are applying (you may apply to only one school)

☒ (4) Arts and Sciences   ☐ (3) Journalism   ☐ (5) Music (see instruction 5)
☐ (2) Education and Social Policy   ☐ (6) Speech   Instrument (principal _____; secondary _____)
(Human Development and Social Policy ___;   ☐ (7) Technological Institute   Voice (alto ___; soprano ___; bass ___; tenor ___; other ___)
Secondary Teacher Training ___)   (engineering)   Five-Year BM/BA ___; Five-Year BM/BS (engineering) ___

25. List several fields of undergraduate study that interest you. Underline the principal field, if known. (School of Speech candidates, indicate department, e.g., radio-television-film, theatre, etc.)   medicine, social work, business

26. Are you interested in applying to one of the following programs? Check the appropriate box. (see instruction 6)

☐ Honors Program in Medical Education (Regular Plan only: see page 7)   ☐ Integrated Science Program (Arts and Sciences candidates only)
☐ Mathematical Methods in the Social Sciences (Arts and Sciences candidates only)

27. If you are considering one or more of the following career areas, please indicate

☒ Business/management   ☐ Dentistry   ☐ Law   ☒ Medicine   ☐ Nursing   ☐ Physical therapy

I certify that to the best of my knowledge all statements by me are correct, complete, and my own. I understand that this application and all other records gathered for my admission files are confidential and will not be disclosed to me, my parents, or any other person, except at the sole discretion of the Dean of Admission, Financial Aid, and Records.

Date   November 15, 1989   Signature   Tova Kohn

This application must be signed by the applicant. The Office of Admission will return any unsigned application.

Northwestern University • Application for Admission   *Part II*

Please check one:
☐ Early Plan   ☒ Regular Plan   ☐ Transfer
    Deadline, November 1   Deadline, January 1

The Admission Committee does not review an application until both Part I and Part II have arrived. You may send them separately. The Office of Admission will acknowledge receipt of Part I only. Send all materials to Office of Admission, Northwestern University, P.O. Box 3060 – 1801 Hinman Avenue, Evanston, Illinois 60204-3060.

Be sure to print your full name on each page you attach. Staple all pages together.

Name	Kohn	Tova	
	last	first	middle

Address	1410 Abbot St.	Lincolnwood	IL	60646
	number and street	city	state	zip

Date of birth	12 15 72	Social Security number	123-45-6789
	month day year		

1. Please provide a list and brief description of important time commitments other than academic work during the last several years (for example: school organizations, jobs, religious groups, the arts, service, athletics, individual interests). Organize this information in a chart.

Name of activity/dates of involvement/position or title/hours per week   What do you do?

Activity/Position	Dates	Hours	Responsibilities
part-time job/ Assistant to Manager, Murray's Supermarket	9/88-present	12 per week	data entry; assist with ordering, stocking, and pricing
nursing home visits	9/88-present	2 per week	talk with residents; send cards and letters to residents; organize annual Christmas party
Spanish Club/ Secretary during senior year	9/86-present	1 per month	attend club meetings and programs; keep minutes of meetings
Student Council/ Class Representative	9/87-5/88	1½ per week	attend weekly meetings; make weekly reports to ten homerooms

Discuss one activity that has been especially important to you.

Of all the activities listed above, the one that has probably been most important to me is my part-time job. I started as a stock girl in the supermarket and after a short time was asked if I'd like to work as a cashier. After one month at the register, I was asked if I would like to learn about computers. When I told the manager that I knew how to use an Apple, he told me to report to the store's office on the second floor when I came into work the next day. I have been learning about ordering and stocking, classifying and pricing, and dealing with wholesalers. This has been very valuable to me because it's given me an introduction to the real world of business. It also has shown me that hard work and honesty can pay off.

(Over)

2. **In the last year or two, what have you done on your own or taken the time to pursue other than school activities? Write about one of these pursuits in detail rather than listing several.**

My grandmother is in a nursing home. Every Sunday we would go to
visit her. I couldn't help but notice how many people never
seemed to have anyone come to see them. I spoke to a nurse at
the home and asked if these people ever had company. When I
heard the sad truth and saw their loneliness, I felt so sad, I
knew I wanted to do something. At first, I would just stop by
and say hello to each one. Then, I mentioned in my English class
one day when we were talking about pen pals that I thought it
would be great if we could write to some of the people at the
home and maybe go to visit them once in a while. At first, only
two people came with me. They told the rest of the class about
their visits and the next week, three more people came. At
Christmas, the class had a party for the residents. Each resident
received a little gift and the gift of a visit from one of the
students. Now we have a "club" of seven people who take turns
visiting the people in the nursing home and sending them cards
and letters, especially on holidays and their birthdays. Even
though they don't always remember us from week to week, they're
so happy when we come to see them that it makes us feel good, so
good I sometimes wonder who is benefiting more from the visits.

3. **If you are not now attending school, why did you discontinue your studies? What have you been doing since leaving school? Answer these questions on an extra page. Please print your full name on it and attach it to the completed Part II.**

4. **Which of the following encouraged your interest in Northwestern University? You may check more than one.**

☐ Student Search Service (College Board)

☐ Family member (Northwestern graduate? ☐ Yes who? _____   ☐ No)

☒ Visit to Northwestern (when? <u>several times</u>)

☐ Interview (where? _____ when? _____)
   If not, do you plan to have one?   ☒ Yes ☐ No   Schedule an interview before your deadline (see instruction 5).

☒ Northwestern student (who? <u>Becky Rauff</u>)

☐ Northwestern graduate, not a family member (who? _____)

☒ Teacher (who? <u>Linda Schinke-Llano</u>)

☐ College day/night program (where? _____ when? _____)

☐ Northwestern off-campus program (where? _____ when? _____)

☐ Northwestern on-campus program (when? _____)

☒ I wrote for information

☐ Other (for example, publications, media); please explain _____

Be sure to include question 5 when you return this page.

Northwestern University • Application for Admission   *Part II*

Name _____Kohn_____Tova_____
                    last   first   middle

5. The Admission Committee values the personal statements that candidates provide. Beyond what you have written in questions 1 and 2, please write about some aspect of your life that is of present, on-going importance to you (300-400 words, a minimum but not a limit). Please discuss why it is important to you. Try to avoid discussing your credentials and achievements. They appear elsewhere in the application and supporting materials.

A few words of advice: Please do not restrict yourself to factual accounts, and do not submit reports or papers written for a class or competition. Avoid writing about singular, out-of-the-ordinary events. Such experiences can be powerful, but they rarely tell the Admission Committee as much about you as comments drawn from everyday life. You should, of course, write whatever you wish to present to the committee; these suggestions are meant to encourage you to do just that.

We urge you not to submit photocopied statements. We appreciate the extra time and effort that original work requires.

Transfer candidates: In addition to this essay, please attach a statement assessing your college experience to date. You may include the reasons for transferring to Northwestern.

There are so many things that are important to me every single day, probably because of my past. Even though I haven't lived that long, I have had the experience of being uprooted from my homeland, of seeing my father have to work in a job that is not what he was trained for in our native country, of seeing my mother go to work in the factory every day to help support us until my father can do the kind of work he should be doing. Because of these experiences, things that are particularly important to me are relationships, respect, and freedom. My mother and father have taught my brothers, my sister, and me that if you do any kind of honest labor, you should not be ashamed, because you are earning your own way. Hard work and hard workers should be respected, and that includes hard workers in school. I know what it feels like to come to a strange country and not know the language or the customs, and to be laughed at because I made stupid mistakes. I can never laugh at anyone whose language or culture or appearance is different from mine because I know what that feels like. We need to stop and think sometimes about the lack of respect we often show for each other. I count freedom as something that is of great importance. If you were born and raised in the United States, you may not appreciate what it is like to be able to go to school, get a part-time job, apply to the school of your choice, even live where you want.

Every day of my life is important to me. Getting good grades in school, earning the trust of my boss at work, having good friends and a wonderful family are especially important. Sure, I worry about college: Can I afford it? Will I be able to make it? All I can do is try my best, and then try a little harder. My daily life is not exciting by other people's standards, but it's all that I can handle right now. Between school, my job, my extracurricular activities, visits to the nursing home, and Saturday night dates, I consider myself a very busy person. The nicest part about being me is that I realize how lucky I am. I want to go to college to fulfill a dream, although I'm not sure yet if it's a dream of being a huge success in the business world or of going into some phase of the medical profession, or maybe even becoming a social worker. I just know I love working with people, but I'd also like to make money.

(continued)

Please sign the application (you may continue your essay on the reverse side).

I certify that to the best of my knowledge all statements submitted by me are correct, complete, and my own. I understand that this application and all other records gathered for my admission files are confidential and will not be disclosed to me, my parents, or any other person, except at the sole discretion of the Dean of Admission, Financial Aid, and Records.

Date *November 15, 1989*   Signature *Tova Kohn*

This application must be signed by the applicant. The Office of Admission will return any unsigned application.

Essay (continued)

    I want to spend my college years studying thought-provoking subjects, meeting diverse people, and participating in a variety of activities. All these experiences will help me find out what I'm good at and what I really enjoy. Then I'll be able to choose the career that's best for me and pull together the various aspects of my present life into a bright, purposeful future.

▶ Procedure

1. If possible, make a copy of the application and use the copy to practice writing your answers. Or, answer all the questions on scrap paper first. Do not write on the original application yet.

2. Read *all* the directions on the application carefully. Ask a guidance counselor, teacher, parent, or anyone else who can help you about anything you don't understand. It is never wrong to say that you don't understand something, even if you think it is probably something very simple.

3. Pay particular attention to directions that tell whether the application must be typed or printed in your own handwriting.

4. Read the directions a second time, following them one by one on your practice copy or scrap paper.

5. After you have practiced answering all the informational questions, print or type your answers on the actual application, making sure to follow directions such as "Last name first." Proofread as you go along. If you're typing, make sure that you have hit the letters you meant to hit and that you are working in the right spaces.

6. Before you begin writing the answer to an essay question, make an outline on scrap paper. (See "Making an Outline," pages 114–124.) Check your outline to be sure that it includes all the information you want and that the information is in the proper sequence.

7. Write your essay on scrap paper, following your outline.

8. Proofread your essay. Make corrections, additions, and/or deletions. Check your spelling, grammar, and punctuation. If possible, ask a teacher or guidance counselor to read your essay before you print or type it on the application form.

9. Type or print your essay(s) on the application.

10. The next day, proofread your application one more time.

11. If possible, have a parent, teacher, or counselor look over your application before you mail it. Be sure you attach any other forms and/or checks that are required.

▶ Practice

Now it's your turn.

TASK: to fill out a college application

SITUATION: You want to apply to a college. You have received the application and must now complete it. Remember, (1) read all the directions first; (2) use scrap paper to practice your answers before you write even your name on the actual application; (3) consult the chapter on "Making an Outline" (pages 114–124) for help with your essay answers; and (4) proofread everything carefully when you're finished.

William Paterson College
Wayne, New Jersey

Application for Admission

Enlightened Minds. Richer Lives.

School of the Arts and Communication
School of Education and Community Service
School of Health Professions and Nursing
School of Humanities
School of Management
School of Science and Mathematics
School of Social Science

Application Information and Instructions

All Applicants
Priority Service

Because of an increase of application growth over the past several years, William Paterson College has experienced unprecedented demand for services to new students. It is now essential that students interested in attending William Paterson College apply for admissions and services (financial aid, scholarships, residence hall space and testing) as early as possible. To encourage early applications, William Paterson College has instituted the Priority Service program.

Under the Priority Service program, students applying for admissions and services for new students by April 15, will receive priority service from participating offices. While April 15 is the priority services date, students may apply much earlier, and they are encouraged to do so.

Application Deadlines

Application and supporting transcripts must be received by the deadlines dates shown below:

	Fall	Spring
Freshman	June 30	November 15
Transfer	August 1	November 15
Second Bachelor Degree	August 1	November 15
Readmit	August 1	November 15

Freshman Students

Admission Requirements:
Freshman candidates are required to have an official high school transcript and SAT or ACT scores sent to the **ADMISSIONS OFFICE.**

High School Record

Applicants are considered eligible if they have taken sixteen (16) Carnegie Units and have demonstrated good academic ability. Your record should show the following courses.

Subject Area	Unit Requirements	
English	4	Composition Literature
Mathematics	3	Algebra I Geometry Algebra II Higher Level Math
Laboratory Science	2	Biology Chemistry Physics

Laboratory science requirements may be chosen from biology, chemistry, physics, earth sciences, or anatomy/physiology.

Social Science	2	American History World History Political Science
Additional College Preparatory Subjects	5	Advanced Math Literature Foreign Language Social Sciences

Certain departments have specific requirements beyond those listed above.

- Students entering mathematics or science are expected to have taken more than the minimum courses in those areas.
- Nursing students need a full year in both Bilogy and Chemistry.
- G.E.D. - If you have a high school equivalency diploma recognized by New Jersey, this may be presented in place of the above requirements.

SAT/ACT Requirements:

Entering freshmen students must have taken the Scholastic Aptitude Test (SAT) or the American College Test (ACT) and have their scores sent to the Admissions Office of William Paterson College. To submit your scores to WPC indicate code **2518** for the SAT and code **2584** for the ACT.

Advance Standing Students

(Transfer, Re-admit, Second Baccalaureate Degree Students).

Transfer Students

William Paterson College accepts students for fall and winter entry (September and January) for full- or part-time study. When applying these students must present at least 12 college-level credits with a minimum 2.0 grade point average; business administration and education majors must have at least a 2.5 GPA. Applicants who have completed fewer than 12 collegiate credits must also submit their high school transcript. There are some limitations on the number of credits accepted, e.g., a maximum of 70 credits from a two-year college, 90 credits from a four-year college. Inquire of our Admissions staff for more details on transferring credits.

1. You must request all colleges previously attended to forward a transcript of all college work completed to the Director of Admissions. The application form should show all courses in progress which will not appear on a transcript as submitted. To insure accurate evaluations, applicants from out-of-state colleges should have appropriate catalogs sent to the Admissions Office.

2. Please include a copy of credit by examination, either CLEP or USAFI.

3. Credit will be transferred if:
   a. The college from which credits are to be transferred is on a list of approved colleges and universities.
   b. They fit into the requirements or curriculum selected.
   c. All post-high school work carries at least a 2.0 (C) cumulative grade point average on a four (4) point scale.

4. Admission decisions are made on a rolling basis. Early application and early submission of all required records is advised as course selection and housing space may be limited or gone before the application deadline.

5. Applicants admitted with 60 credits *must* declare a major and be accepted by a major department.

6. If you have completed less than 12 transferable credits, you MUST submit SAT scores and an official high school transcript.

Note: Failure to submit complete official records of all prior college coursework and high school transcripts when required, will result in a delay in the application review process.

Page 2

Re-Admit Students

Students who have completed undergraduate courses at WPC must file this application. If college courses have been completed at another college or university, an official copy of the transcript(s) must be forwarded to the WPC Admissions Office. Certain college policies may require you to complete an additional form and/or supply further information resulting in a delay of the admissions process. Please submit your application and all required documents as early as possible.

Second Baccalaureate Degree at William Paterson College

Students who already hold a baccalaureate degree may obtain a second baccalaureate degree in any non-teaching program. Applicants are considered upper-level division students and pay undergraduate fees. All credits earned through this program appear as undergraduate credits on the student's transcript. Students must complete all major requirements and collateral courses. A minimum of 30 credits must be completed at William Paterson College while enrolled in this program. Nursing major students must have completed the freshman requirements in order to be eligible for sophomore status in nursing.

Special Admission

Educational Opportunity Fund Program (EOF):
The Educational Opportunity Fund program (EOF) is a special admissions and support program for students who are educationally underprepared and financially disadvantaged. The program is designed to provide full financial support and a broad range of educational and counseling assistance for all eligible students.

The program offers students the opportunity to begin their college experience in a summer program organized to assist students to become familiar with the academic demands of higher education, to strengthen basic skills and to gain exposure to the campus and college life. The EOF program also assists students in their personal and social adjustment to college.

To be eligible, students must have been residents of New Jersey for the past year, have a gross family income which meets state criteria and demonstrate potential for academic success. Additional information on page 6.

Early Admission: This program is available for highly motivated and academically exceptional students who have completed their junior year of high school and seek college admission. They may submit an application for early admission provided they meet the following criteria: 1) combined SAT scores of 1,000 or higher (or equivalent PSAT scores) and/or rank in the top 10% of their class, and/or exhibit exceptional talent in a special area; 2) receive the endorsement of a teacher or counselor; 3) submit a written essay describing their reasons for seeking early admission.

Non-Traditional Students: Students who have not completed any college coursework and are 21 or older or have been out of high school for 2 years or more are considered non-traditional students. They must submit a high school transcript indicating graduation or copies of GED scores and diploma to be evaluated. An interview may be necessary before a decision is made.

Adult Students: Within the William Paterson College community there are a large number of adult or non-traditional students. Some are returning to school after a time lapse, some are taking courses to directly support their careers, and others come for personal enrichment. Most attend on a part-time basis with classes in the day, evening or on Saturday. The Center for Continuing Education works in conjunction with other administrative offices to provide support services for these students. For further information call (201) 595-2346.

International Students: Applicants from other countries are welcome at WPC. Admissions is based on a review of the appropriate educational documents as well as proficiency in the English language as measured by the Test of English as a Foreign Language (TOEFL). To receive more detailed international student information you may call or write.

International Admissions Officer
Admissions Office
William Paterson College
Wayne, NJ 07470
Telephone (201) 595-2763

Advanced Placement

Some highly qualified entering freshmen may wish to take advanced level courses. This is acceptable if the student has an outstanding score in the appropriate subject in tests of either the CEEB or the College Board Achievement tests.

Eligibility for advanced placement may be established on the basis of scores on the Advanced Placement Exam. *·ion of the College Board, College Level Examination Prog. (CLEP), or challenge examinations.

Veterans

Certain courses taken while enlisted in the Armed Services may be used towards the WPC bachelor degree. Veterans must submit a notarized copy of the DD214 or DD295 and official copies of high school and college transcripts along with the application. Contact the Admissions Office for detailed information.

Scholarships and Financial Aid.

Academic merit scholarships are offered to incoming freshmen. They are the Academic Excellence Scholarships and the Minority Student Scholarships. These scholarships are based not on need, but on academic performance. For a scholarship application please call (201) 595-2126.

Financial Aid is available from state and federally funded programs. Distribution of funds (grants, loans, and college work study) are based on need. Information and applications are available from the Financial Aid Office: (201) 595-2202.

Statement of Policy

William Paterson College is an EEO/AA employer and does not discriminate on the basis of sex, race, religion, color, national origin or handicapping conditions in its admissions, employment and education programs or activities.

APPLICATION FOR UNDERGRADUATE ADMISSION
(Enclose a $10.00 application fee — money order or check)
WILLIAM PATERSON COLLEGE, WAYNE, NJ 07470

Complete All Items (Print in Ink or Type)

1. **Name in full** _____
   Last   First   Middle Initial

   Give name in full. Do not use nicknames or abbreviations

   Important: Indicate any other last name under which transcripts may be received _____

2. **Social Security Number**

   [ ][ ][ ] [ ][ ] [ ][ ][ ][ ]

3. **Home Address**

   _____
   Number and Street

   _____
   City   State   Zip

4. **Country** _____

5. **Phone No.** _____

6. **County** _____ **Code** _____ (see code sheet)

7. **Are you a New Jersey Resident?** [ ] Yes   [ ] No

8. **Date of Birth** _____ _____ _____
   Month   Day   Year

9. **Sex:** [ ] Male   [ ] Female

10. **Please indicate your ethnic background (Required for federal reporting)**

    [ ] Hispanic (H)   [ ] Black (B)   [ ] American Indian or Alaskan Native (I)

    [ ] Asian or Pacific Islander (O)   [ ] Caucasian/All other (W)

11. **Are you a citizen of the U.S.?** [ ] Yes   [ ] No

12. **If no, what is your country of citizenship?** _____

13. **If you are not a U.S. citizen, what type of visa do you hold?** _____

14. **Are you a permanent resident?** [ ] Yes   [ ] No

    Alien Registration #: _____

15. **Are you a veteran?** [ ] Yes   [ ] No

16. **Term: What semester do you plan to enroll?**

    _____ September (4), 19 _____,   _____ January (1), 19 _____

17. **Application type:** (check one)   **Status:** (check one)

    [ ] New Freshman   [ ] Transfer   [ ] Full Time

    [ ] Re-Admit   [ ] Second BA   [ ] Part-Time

Do Not Write in This Box

INFO. REQ.	DATE	DATE	DATE

APP FEE	DATE

DEPOSIT FEE	DATE

I		II				III					IV
Eng	Alg	Geom	Alg II	Trig	Adv. Math	Bio	Chem	Phy	Ear Sci	Other	For Lang

V			VI	OTAL
Am History	World History	Govern-ment	Additonal Academics	Units

H.S. RANK	CLASS SIZE	PERCENTILE
SAT DATE	MATH	VERBAL
SAT DATE	MATH	VERBAL
GED DATE	SCORE	EOF READING

ACADEMIC INDEX	TOEFL

ACCEPT CRITERIA

COMMENTS:

ADMISSIONS OFFICER	DATE

Page 4

18. Selecting your major
From the major code lists on Pages 7 and 8, please indicate your major, major code and concentration code (where required) in the spaces provided

Major _____ Major Code _____ Concentration Code _____

19. Teacher Certification
Secondary education certification is available to students selecting majors marked with an asterisk (*).
Are you interested in incorporating teacher certification with your chosen major?   [ ] YES   [ ] NO

20. What is your family's annual income? (Please see income codes) _____

21. Will you be applying for campus housing?   [ ] YES   [ ] NO

22. Academic History High School _____ _____ _____
　　　　　　　　　　　　　　　　　　　Name of School　　　　　　　　　City　　　　　　　State

High School CEEB #: _____ Date of Graduation: _____

Counselor's Name _____ Phone # _____

Are you presently attending or have you previously attended any college or university? ☐ Yes ☐ No If so, list institutions, locations and dates.
Important: Failure to provide a list of all colleges attended (including correspondence and extension courses) may result in delay in admission, loss of transfer credit, and/or dismissal. It is the applicant's responsibility to have official transcripts forwarded from each college attended. An official report is required even though attendance was for a brief time and no credit was established.

Please list in descending order beginning with current or most recent college

DO NOT WRITE IN THESE BOXES

Name of Institution	Address (City and State)	CEEB #	Term Begin (Mo. & Yr.)	Term End (Mo. & Yr.)	Official Transcript Received	No. of Credits	GPA

Please use additional sheet if necessary

23. High School/College Coursework in progress
Complete this section if you are currently enrolled in high school or college. List all current and future coursework you will complete before your enrollment at William Paterson College.

Name of High School/College	Complete Course Title	Term/Yr.	Units/Credits

If you are not attending a school at the present time, please attach an explanation stating how you have been occupied since your last enrollment in school. Give brief details and dates.

24. I, the undersigned, state that the answers I have given to the questions in this application are complete and true. I agree to abide by the rules and regulations of William Paterson College.

Date _____

_____
Signature of Applicant

Return To: Office of Admissions
The William Paterson College
300 Pompton Road
Wayne, New Jersey 07470

Page 5

William Paterson College

Educational Opportunity Fund (EOF)

The Educational Opportunity Fund offers special admissions consideration to students who show academic promise yet lack the educational and economic means for admission through traditional procedures. Educational support (tutorial) services as well as counseling are provided by the Program. EOF also offers students the opportunity to begin their college experience in a summer enrichment program designed to familiarize students with the academic demands of higher education, strengthen their basic skills, an assist students in adjusting to college life.

To apply for admission to William Paterson College through the Educational Opportunity Fund, you must meet specific academic and income requirements, be a U.S. citizen or permanent resident, and be a New Jersey resident for the last twelve (12) months.

If you wish to be considered for admission through the EOF program or receive more information please complete this supplemental form. If you have any questions please call (201) 595-2181.

Income Eligibility Criteria 1988-1989

Dependent Students Household Size	Gross Income
2 persons	$15,050
3 persons	$17,110
4 persons	$19,170
5 persons	$21,230
6 persons	$23,290
7 persons	$25,350

Add $2,060 for each additional dependent.
UMPC $625 (or less)

Independent Students Household Size	Gross Income
1 including student	$ 9,180
2 persons	$10,240
3 persons	$13,300
4 persons	$15,360

Add $2,060 for each additional dependent.

NAME: _____
           LAST   FIRST   MIDDLE I.
SOCIAL SECURITY # _____

ADDRESS: _____
              STREET

           CITY   STATE   ZIP   COUNTY
PHONE # (   ) _____

☐ New Freshman   ☐ EOF Transfer   Career
                            From: _____   Choice _____
HIGH SCHOOL: _____
DATE OF GRADUATION: _____
INCOME: (SEE CODE SHEET) _____
Are you a U.S. Citizen?   ☐ Yes   ☐ No
Are you a permanent resident?   ☐ Yes   ☐ No
Alien registration # _____
Are you a New Jersey resident? (you must have lived in New Jersey for
the past twelve (12) consecutive months) ☐ Yes   ☐ No

Page 6

WILLIAM PATERSON COLLEGE

CODE LISTS

COUNTY CODES

Atlantic - 01	Monmouth - 13
Bergen - 02	Morris - 14
Burlington - 03	Ocean - 15
Camdem - 04	Passaic - 16
Cape May - 05	Salem - 17
Cumberland - 06	Somerset - 18
Essex - 07	Sussex - 19
Gloucester - 08	Union - 20
Hudson - 09	Warren - 21
Hunterdon - 10	New York - 30
Mercer - 11	Pennsylvania - 40
Middlesex - 12	Other - 50

COMBINED FAMILY INCOME CODE

CODE	INCOME RANGE
0	Less than $10,000
1	Between $10,001 and $12,000
2	Between $12,001 and $13,000
3	Between $13,001 and $15,000
4	Between $15,001 and $20,000
5	Between $20,001 and $25,000
6	Between $25,001 and $30,000
7	Between $30,001 and $35,000
8	Over $35,000

UNDERGRADUATE MAJORS AND CODES

Find your intended major on the list below. Write the name of the major, the assigned major code and the concentration code in the space provided on the undergraduate application. Please note that every major does not have a concentration code. Call the admissions Hot Line for assistance and any questions you may have concerning the application process: (201) 595-2125. For your convenience, three samples have been provided.

1. Major: Biology
    Major Code: 01-B10-BS

2. Major: Early Childhood Ed./English
    Major Code: 04-EC-BA   Concentration Code: ENG

3. Major: Undecided (No major selected)
    Major Code: 06-UND—UND   Concentration Code: UND

Note: Secondary education certification is available to students selecting majors marked with an asterisk (*).

SCHOOL OF THE ARTS AND COMMUNICATION

Major	Major Code	Concentration Code	Major	Major Code	Concentration Code
*Art - History	00-ART-BA	HIST	Jazz Stds. Perf - Wind		
*Art - Studio	00-ART-BA	STDO	Mallet/Guitar	00-MUS-BM	JSW
Fine Arts & Design	00-ART-BFA		Jazz Stds. & Perf - Keyboard	00-MUS-BM	JSK
*Communication	00-COMM-BA		Jazz Stds. Perf - Vocal	00-MUS-BM	JSV
Music Classical Performance	00-MUS-BM	CLS	Theater	00-DRA-BA	
*Music Classical Perf. Vocal	00-MUS-BM	VCE	Liberal Studies/Arts	00-LBST-BA	
*Music Classical Perf. Instr.	00-MUS-BM	INST	and Communications		
Music Management	00-MUS-BM	MGT	Undeclared Arts and		
Musical Studies	00-MUS-BA	STDS	Communications	00-UND-UND	
Jazz Stds. Perf - Drum set	00-MUS-BM	JSD			

Page 7

SCHOOL OF EDUCATION AND COMMUNITY SERVICE

Major	Major Code	Concentration Code
¹ELEMENTARY EDUCATION		
African & Afro-Amer. Studs.	04-ELED-BA	AAAS
Art - History	04-ELED-BA	HIST
Art - Studio	04-ELED-BA	STDO
Biology	04-ELED-BA	BIO
Chemistry	04-ELED-BA	CHEM
Environmental Studies	04-ELED-BA	ENV
French	04-ELED-BA	FR
English - Literature	04-ELED-BA	LIT
English - Writing	04-ELED-BA	WRIT
Geography	04-ELED-BA	GEO
History	04-ELED-BA	HIST
Mathematics	04-ELED-BA	MATH
Philosophy	04-ELED-BA	PHIL
Political Science	04-ELED-BA	POL
Psychology	04-ELED-BA	PSY
Sociology	04-ELED-BA	SOC
Spanish	04-ELED-BA	SPAN
Liberal Stds. Arts & Comm.	04-ELED-BA	LSA
Liberal Stds. Humanities	04-ELED-BA	LSH
Liberal Stds. Soc. Behav. Sci	04-ELED-BA	LSS
Liberal Stds. Math & Nat. Sci.	04-ELED-BA	LSM
¹EARLY CHILDHOOD		
African & Afro-Amer. Studs.	04-EC-BA	AAAS
Art - History	04-EC-BA	HIST
Art - Studio	04-EC-BA	STDO
Biology	04-EC-BA	BIO
Chemistry	04-EC-BA	CHEM
Environmental Studies	04-EC-BA	ENV
English - Literature	04-EC-BA	LIT
English - Writing	04-EC-BA	WRIT
French	04-EC-BA	FR
Geography	04-EC-BA	GEO
History	04-EC-BA	HIST
Mathematics	04-EC-BA	MATH
Philosophy	04-EC-BA	PHIL
Political Science	04-EC-BA	POL
Psychology	04-EC-BA	PSY
Sociology	04-EC-BA	SOC
Spanish	04-EC-BA	SPAN
Liberal Stds./Arts & Comm.	04-EC-BA	LSA
Liberal Stds./Humanities	04-EC-BA	LSH
Liberal Stds./Soc. Behav. Sci	04-EC-BA	LSS
Liberal Stds./Math & Nat. Sci.	04-EC-BA	LSM

¹ Note: Students must have an academic sequence to be an Elementary Education or Early Childhood major.

SPECIAL EDUCATION

Major	Major Code	
*SPECIAL EDUCATION	04-SPED-BA	

MOVEMENT SCIENCE, LEISURE STUDIES.

Major	Major Code	Concentration Code
*Movement Sci. & Leisure Studies	04-MSLS-BS	
Aquatics	04-MSLS-BS	AQA
Adapted Physical Ed.	04-MSLS-BS	ADP
Coaching & Officiating	04-MSLS-BS	CHOF
Dance	04-MSLS-BS	DNCE
Exercise Physiology	04-MSLS-BS	EXP
Recreation & Leisure Stds.	04-MSLS-BS	RCLS
Athletic Training	04-MSLS-BS	ATR

UNDECLARED	**Major Code**	
Undeclared (Education)	04-UND-UND	

SCHOOL OF HEALTH PROFESSIONS AND NURSING

Major	Major Code	Concentration Code
*Health Science (Community Health)	05-CSH-BS	
Nursing	05-NUR-BS	
*Communication Disorders	05-CODS-BA	
Undeclared (Health Professions)	05-UND-UND	
Undeclared (Pre-Nursing)	05-UND-UND	NUR

SCHOOL OF HUMANITIES

Major	Major Code	Concentration Code
*African & Afro-Amer. Stds	03-AAAS-BA	
*English Literature	03-ENG-BA	LIT
*English Writing	03-ENG-BA	WRIT
*French	03-FR-BA	
*History	03-HIST-BA	
Philosophy	03-PHIL-BA	
*Spanish	03-SPAN-BA	
Liberal Studies/Humanities	03-LBST-BA	
Undeclared-Humanities	03-UND-UND	

SCHOOL OF MANAGEMENT

Major	Major Code	Concentration Code
Business Admin. Finance	07-BUS-BA	FIN
Business Admin. Management	07-BUS-BA	MGT
Business Admin. Marketing	07-BUS-BA	MKT
Accounting	07-ACCT-BA	
Economics	07-ECON-BA	
Computer Science	07-CS-BS	
Undeclared/Management	07-UND-UND	

SCHOOL OF SCIENCE AND MATHEMATICS

Major	Major Code	Concentration Code
*Bilogy	01-BIO-BS	
*Chemistry	01-CHEM-BS	
Environmental Studies	01-ENV-BA	
*Mathematics	01-MATH-BA	
*Applied Math/Social Science	01-MATH-BA	APL
*Applied Math/Natural Science	01-MATH-BA	ANS
*Actuarial Math	01-MATH-BA	ACT
Liberal Studies/Math and Natural Science	01-LBST-BA	
Undeclared Science	01-UND-UND	

SCHOOL OF SOCIAL SCIENCE

Major	Major Code	Concentration Code
*Geography	02-GEO-BA	
*Political Science	02-POL-BA	
Psychology	02-PSY-BA	
*Sociology/Anthropology	02-SOC-BA	
Sociology/Anthropology/ Criminal Justice	02-SOC-BA	CJA
Liberal Studies/Social Behavior Science	02-LBST-BA	
Undeclared Social Science	02-UND-UND	

NO MAJOR SELECTED

Major	Major Code	Concentration Code
Undecided	06-UND-UND	UND

CHAPTER 11
Filling Out a Job Application

There may be one or many job applications in your future. Very few people go through life without ever having to fill out a job application. Filling out a job application is not a difficult thing to do, but doing it right is extremely important.

▷▷ Rationale

Job applications ask for all the information employers want to know about people before deciding whether to interview them. The way you answer the questions on the job application may determine whether or not you are called for an interview or considered for a job. Therefore, it is important to know how to fill out an application correctly.

Note: Federal (United States) laws prohibit employers from requiring job applicants to answer certain questions. These include questions about age, race, sex, marital status, dependents, and other questions of a personal nature. If these questions appear on an application, you must decide whether to answer them or not. Some companies, especially those directly involved with the government, are allowed to ask these questions for a variety of security reasons, but most employers today are careful to use applications that protect the rights and privacy of people applying for jobs.

▷▷ Materials Needed

pen, practice paper, job application, dictionary, information about your educational background and work experience, names and addresses of references

Skills Involved

reading comprehension, spelling, neat and legible handwriting, compiling and organizing information

Important Vocabulary

compiling collecting

dependents people who rely on someone else for support. Children and others who can't work or earn money are dependents.

employee a person who works for someone else

employer a company or person for whom others work

hiring giving someone a job

marital status whether you are married, single, divorced, or widowed

personal relating to your private life. Your marital status is personal information; your job skills are not.

references people who know you and can provide information about your qualifications and the kind of person you are

Example

See next page.

APPLICATION FOR EMPLOYMENT
(PRE-EMPLOYMENT QUESTIONNAIRE)   (AN EQUAL OPPORTUNITY EMPLOYER)

PERSONAL INFORMATION

DATE 12/1/90

NAME Stein Suzanne E.
LAST   FIRST   MIDDLE

SOCIAL SECURITY NUMBER 111-11-1111

PRESENT ADDRESS 8 Elm St. Brownsville TX 78520
STREET   CITY   STATE   ZIP

PERMANENT ADDRESS same as above
STREET   CITY   STATE   ZIP

PHONE NO. 555-6666   ARE YOU 18 YEARS OR OLDER Yes ☒   No ☐

SPECIAL QUESTIONS

DO NOT ANSWER **ANY** OF THE QUESTIONS IN THIS FRAMED AREA UNLESS THE EMPLOYER HAS **CHECKED** A **BOX PRECEDING** A QUESTION, THEREBY INDICATING THAT THE INFORMATION IS REQUIRED FOR A BONA FIDE OCCUPATIONAL QUALIFICATION, OR DICTATED BY NATIONAL SECURITY LAWS, OR IS NEEDED FOR OTHER LEGALLY PERMISSIBLE REASONS.

☐ Height _____ feet _____ inches

☐ Weight _____ lbs.

☐ What Foreign Languages do you speak fluently? _____ Read _____ Write _____

☐ _____

☐ Citizen of U.S. _____ Yes _____ No

☐ Date of Birth* _____

*The Age Discrimination in Employment Act of 1967 prohibits discrimination on the basis of age with respect to individuals who are at least 40 but less than 70 years of age.

EMPLOYMENT DESIRED

POSITION salesperson   DATE YOU CAN START 1/3/91   SALARY DESIRED open

ARE YOU EMPLOYED NOW? yes   IF SO MAY WE INQUIRE OF YOUR PRESENT EMPLOYER? yes

EVER APPLIED TO THIS COMPANY BEFORE? no   WHERE? ——   WHEN? ——

EDUCATION	NAME AND LOCATION OF SCHOOL	*NO. OF YEARS ATTENDED	*DID YOU GRADUATE?	SUBJECTS STUDIED
GRAMMAR SCHOOL	No. 6 School, Carrol St., Paterson, NJ	8	yes	
HIGH SCHOOL	Brownsville High School Brownsville, TX	4	yes	English, science, math, business
COLLEGE				
TRADE, BUSINESS OR CORRESPONDENCE SCHOOL	Haley's Correspondence School for Sales, Chicago, IL	1	yes	how to be a top salesperson

*The Age Discrimination in Employment Act of 1967 prohibits discrimination on the basis of age with respect to individuals who are at least 40 but less than 70 years of age.

GENERAL

SUBJECTS OF SPECIAL STUDY OR RESEARCH WORK sales

U.S. MILITARY OR NAVAL SERVICE ——   RANK ——   PRESENT MEMBERSHIP IN NATIONAL GUARD OR RESERVES ——

TOPS FORM 3285 (REVISED)   (CONTINUED ON OTHER SIDE)   LITHO IN U.S.A.

Used with permission of TOPS Business Forms, 111 Marquardt Drive, Wheeling, Illinois 60090.

FORMER EMPLOYERS [LIST BELOW LAST FOUR EMPLOYERS, STARTING WITH LAST ONE FIRST].

DATE MONTH AND YEAR	NAME AND ADDRESS OF EMPLOYER	SALARY	POSITION	REASON FOR LEAVING
FROM Sept. 1988 TO present	Jones Department Store 1 Main St., Brownsville, TX	$15,000	sales	to improve and advance
FROM TO				
FROM TO				
FROM TO				

REFERENCES: GIVE THE NAMES OF THREE PERSONS NOT RELATED TO YOU, WHOM YOU HAVE KNOWN AT LEAST ONE YEAR.

NAME	ADDRESS	BUSINESS	YEARS ACQUAINTED
1 Rev. C. Smythe	15 Elmora Rd. Brownsville, TX	clergy	10
2 Mr. R. Jones	Jones Dept. Store 1 Main St., Brownsville, TX	owner	2
3 Mrs. J. Méndez	555 6th Ave. Brownsville, TX	store manager	2

PHYSICAL RECORD:

DO YOU HAVE ANY PHYSICAL LIMITATIONS THAT PRECLUDE YOU FROM PERFORMING ANY WORK FOR WHICH YOU ARE BEING CONSIDERED? ☐ Yes ☒ No

PLEASE DESCRIBE:

IN CASE OF EMERGENCY NOTIFY Mr. J. Stein 8 Elm St., Brownsville, TX 555-6666
NAME   ADDRESS   PHONE NO.

"I CERTIFY THAT THE FACTS CONTAINED IN THIS APPLICATION ARE TRUE AND COMPLETE TO THE BEST OF MY KNOWLEDGE AND UNDERSTAND THAT, IF EMPLOYED, FALSIFIED STATEMENTS ON THIS APPLICATION SHALL BE GROUNDS FOR DISMISSAL.

I AUTHORIZE INVESTIGATION OF ALL STATEMENTS CONTAINED HEREIN AND THE REFERENCES LISTED ABOVE TO GIVE YOU ANY AND ALL INFORMATION CONCERNING MY PREVIOUS EMPLOYMENT AND ANY PERTINENT INFORMATION THEY MAY HAVE, PERSONAL OR OTHERWISE, AND RELEASE ALL PARTIES FROM ALL LIABILITY FOR ANY DAMAGE THAT MAY RESULT FROM FURNISHING SAME TO YOU.

I UNDERSTAND AND AGREE THAT, IF HIRED, MY EMPLOYMENT IS FOR NO DEFINITE PERIOD AND MAY, REGARDLESS OF THE DATE OF PAYMENT OF MY WAGES AND SALARY, BE TERMINATED AT ANY TIME WITHOUT ANY PRIOR NOTICE."

DATE 12/1/90 SIGNATURE Suzanne E. Stein

DO NOT WRITE BELOW THIS LINE

INTERVIEWED BY   DATE

HIRED: ☐ Yes ☐ No   POSITION   DEPT.

SALARY/WAGE   DATE REPORTING TO WORK

APPROVED: 1.   2.   3.
EMPLOYMENT MANAGER   DEPT. HEAD   GENERAL MANAGER

This form has been designed to strictly comply with State and Federal fair employment practice laws prohibiting employment discrimination. This Application for Employment Form is sold for general use throughout the United States. TOPS assumes no responsibility for the inclusion in said form of any questions which, when asked by the Employer of the Job Applicant, may violate State and/or Federal Law.

▶ Procedure

1. Read the application carefully. Be sure to follow the directions.

a. Use a pen to fill in your answers (unless you are asked to type).

b. Look up any words you don't understand in a dictionary or ask someone to explain their meaning. Never be ashamed to say you don't understand something.

2. If there are any questions that require a paragraph or longer answer, write your answer on separate paper first so you can correct it before you put it on the application.

3. Look at the example application again. Notice these important details and watch for them whenever you fill out an application:

a. *Name:* Last name is asked for first.

b. *Address:* If you are presently living or staying somewhere other than at your permanent address, be sure to include that information. Your present address is necessary for an employer to get in touch with you to set up an interview.

c. *Special Questions:* Follow the directions, and don't answer these questions unless you are specifically asked to do so.

d. *Employment Desired:* If you don't want your present employer to know you are looking for another job, ask that he or she not be contacted—at least until you have been interviewed and there is a possibility you will be hired.

If you are not sure what salary you want, or if you want to hear what's available, write *open* in the *salary desired* blank. That means you are willing to discuss this item with the interviewer.

e. *Education:* Notice that the years you attended or graduated from particular schools are not asked for, just the *number* of years you attended each school. This protects you from revealing your age.

f. *Former Employers:* Be sure to follow the directions and to put your most recent employer first. When listing reasons for leaving a job, it is always best to be positive: you are seeking to improve yourself, your salary, etc. Personal motives such as not getting along with your boss are not good reasons in the eyes of future employers.

g. Draw a line through any spaces that don't apply to you to show that you have read the question but that it doesn't apply to you.

h. Read everything carefully before you sign the application, and be sure you understand what you are agreeing to.

 Practice

Now it's your turn.

TASK: to fill out a job application

SITUATION: You are applying for a job of your choice. Fill out the following application. Remember to read it first and be sure you understand everything before filling it in.

APPLICATION FOR EMPLOYMENT

(PRE-EMPLOYMENT QUESTIONNAIRE)   **(AN EQUAL OPPORTUNITY EMPLOYER)**

Date _____

Name [Last Name First] _____   Soc. Sec. No. _____

Address _____   Telephone _____

What kind of work are you applying for? _____

What special qualifications do you have? _____

What office machines can you operate? _____

Are you 18 years or older?   Yes _____   No _____

SPECIAL PURPOSE QUESTIONS

DO NOT ANSWER **ANY** OF THE QUESTIONS IN THIS FRAMED AREA UNLESS THE EMPLOYER HAS **CHECKED A BOX PRECEDING** A QUESTION, THEREBY INDICATING THAT THE INFORMATION IS REQUIRED FOR A BONA FIDE OCCUPATIONAL QUALIFICATION, OR DICTATED BY NATIONAL SECURITY LAWS, OR IS NEEDED FOR OTHER LEGALLY PERMISSIBLE REASONS.

☐ Height ___ Feet ___ Inches ☐ Weight ___ Lbs. ☐ Are you prevented from lawfully becoming employed in the U.S.? Yes ___ No ___

☐ Have you been convicted of a felony or misdemeanor within the last 5 years?* Yes ___ No ___ Describe _____

*You will not be denied employment solely because of a conviction record, unless the offense is related to the job for which you have applied.

MILITARY SERVICE RECORD

Armed Forces Service _____ Yes _____ No

Branch of Service _____ Duties _____

Rank or rating at time of enlistment _____ Rating at time of discharge_____

Do you have any physical limitations that prohibit you from performing any work for which you are being considered?   Yes ___ No ___

If yes, what can be done to accommodate your limitation? Describe _____

EDUCATION

SCHOOL	*NO. OF YEARS ATTENDED	NAME OF SCHOOL	CITY	COURSE	*DID YOU GRADUATE?
GRAMMAR					
HIGH					
COLLEGE					
OTHER					

*The Age Discrimination in Employment Act of 1967 prohibits discrimination on the basis of age with respect to individuals who are at least 40 but less than 70 years of age.

EXPERIENCE

NAME AND ADDRESS OF COMPANY	DATE FROM	DATE TO	LIST YOUR DUTIES	STARTING SALARY	FINAL SALARY	REASON FOR LEAVING

BUSINESS REFERENCES

NAME	ADDRESS	OCCUPATION

This form has been designed to strictly comply with State and Federal fair employment practice laws prohibiting employment discrimination. This Application for Employment Form is sold for general use throughout the United States. TOPS assumes no responsibility for the inclusion in said form of any questions which, when asked by the Employer of the Job Applicant, may violate State and/or Federal Law.

TOPS Form 3286 (84-3)   Litho in U.S.A.

Used with permission of TOPS Business Forms, 111 Marquardt Drive, Wheeling, Illinois 60090.

CHAPTER 12
Writing a Résumé

A résumé is a summary of your qualifications—in particular, your work experience and educational background. Your first job, an "entry-level" job, may not require a résumé. However, as you increase your skills and work experience and look for jobs that will allow you to earn more money, you may want or need to send a résumé to potential employers.

▷▷ Rationale

People in charge of hiring employees usually ask for a résumé from job applicants and then contact the applicants whose résumés show the best qualifications for the type of job involved. If your résumé shows that you have the skills and background an employer is looking for, and if it's neat and professional in appearance, you may be asked to go in for an interview.

Note: As you go from job to job, it's a good idea to keep a record of the exact names and addresses of the places you've worked, who your supervisor(s) were, and the dates of your employment there. This makes it easier to keep your résumé up to date.

▷▷ Materials Needed

typewriter or word processor; unlined paper; access to a copying machine; names, addresses, dates of places you've worked and schools you've attended; practice paper; pen or pencil

▷▷ Skills Involved

typing or word processing; organizing material; planning a layout for a résumé; using correct spelling, punctuation, and capitalization

Important Vocabulary

employee a person who works for someone else

employer a company or person for whom others work

employment a job

entry-level beginning level; requiring little or no experience

layout a plan for the way something will look

marital status whether you are married, single, divorced, or widowed

personnel department the department in a company that is responsible for hiring, firing, and dealing with employee benefits and problems

potential possible

references people who know you and can provide information about your qualifications and the kind of person you are

supervisor a person in charge of other employees

Example
See next page.

OLGA ORTIZ
400 Lane Drive
Albany, New York 12234
518-555-1234

CAREER OBJECTIVE

Full-time position as a bilingual aide/teacher in a public school.

WORK EXPERIENCE

Sept. 1987–Present   Bilingual Aide   Marsh Adult School
                                                    1 Market St.
                                                    Albany, NY 12234

Work with new Spanish-speaking arrivals, helping them to register for
English classes.

EDUCATION

June 1987:   AA Degree   Passaic County Community College
                               College Blvd.
                               Paterson, NJ 07501

June 1985:   Diploma   Passaic High School
                               Passaic, NJ 07055

HONORS AND ACTIVITIES

Certificate of Merit in Spanish (Passaic High School)
Perfect Attendance Award (Passaic High School)
President, French Club (Passaic County Community College)

SKILLS

Multilingual (fluent in English, Spanish, and French)

REFERENCES

Mr. K. Bodnar, Chair   Prof. L. Smith
English Dept.   Passaic County Community College
Passaic High School   College Blvd.
Passaic, NJ 07055   Paterson, NJ 07501

Dr. J. Mendez, Director
Marsh Adult School
1 Market St.
Albany, NY 12234

▶ Procedure

There are many acceptable ways to write a résumé. The format (layout) used here is one popular style that is easy to read, is pleasing to look at, and contains the necessary information. The laws of the United States protect you from having to state your marital status, age, number of dependents, race, color, or sex on your résumé.

1. At the top of the paper, center your name, address, telephone number, and, if you wish, your social security number. Use single spacing as shown below. (A résumé should always be typed, typeset, or done on a word processor.)

```
                    Donald Lovrin
                 109 Simpson Blvd.
              Los Angeles, CA  90024
                  (213) 555-6782
```

2. Leave some blank space, then type CAREER OBJECTIVE at the left side of the paper. Under it, write the goal you'd like to reach, the job you'd really like to have.

3. Leave some blank space, then type WORK EXPERIENCE at the left side of the paper. List all the jobs you've had, beginning with your most recent job experience and working backwards. Leave a blank space between the entries. Naturally, if you have had only one job, you will report only that one. There are three important items to include in each entry:

a. the date you started the job and the date you stopped working at the job. (If you still work there, use *present* for the second date.)

b. your job title and the name and address of your employer. (If you worked for a specific person whom you would like the reader to contact, include his or her name.)

c. a brief description of your responsibilities.

WORK EXPERIENCE

November 1987–present   Stage Manager
                                         Whoop-De-Doo Productions
                                         1111 Wilship Blvd.
                                         Los Angeles, CA   90024

In charge of all television shows, making sure everything
needed for the television sets is ready for the camera
operators, supervising the people on the set, working with the
directors of the various shows.

July 1985–October 1987   Stagehand
                                         Short Subjects
                                         Dabney Studios
                                         Miller Mall
                                         Los Angeles, CA   90023

Worked for stage manager, gathering props for TV
productions, getting sets ready, doing whatever was needed as
I learned the business.

4. Leave at least two blank spaces after this section and type
EDUCATION at the left side of your paper. List all the schools you've
attended, starting with your most recent educational experience and
working back. You don't have to include anything before high school
unless you have had some unusual educational training. In each entry,
include the date you received any degree or diploma from the school,
the type of degree you obtained, and the name and address of the
school. If you attended a school but never received any degree or
diploma, write the date you started at the school and the date you
left, the same way you wrote the dates for your work experience.

EDUCATION

Sept. 1983–June 1985   TV Camera and Professional Inst.
                            25 Fount Ave.
                            Hollywood, CA   90027

June 1983 Diploma   St. Mary's High School
                            Hollywood Ave.
                            Hollywood, CA   90027

5. If you have received any awards, prizes, or certificates in any of your classes, or if you have participated in any clubs, teams, or other school activities, be sure to include them here. They show that you are an active member of your school. Type HONORS AND ACTIVITIES at the left side of your paper. Look at how Olga Ortiz listed her honors and activities in the example on page 106.

6. If you have any special skills or training that might help you get the kind of job you're looking for, include those next. Type SKILLS at the left side of your paper, leaving at least two blank spaces after the previous section. Briefly describe whatever these special skills are, just as Olga Ortiz did in the example résumé on page 106.

7. Leave at least two blank spaces below your last entry and type REFERENCES at the left side of the paper. Then give the names and addresses of two or three people who can provide information about you and your qualifications. The easiest way to list the information is the way you would address an envelope. Be sure to include each person's position or title so the reader can see how these people would know about your abilities.

REFERENCES

Ms. Deborah Leschin, TV Producer
1111 Studio St.
Studio City, CA   91604

Mr. Michael Boggs, Cameraman
4376 Wayne St.
Hollywood, CA   90023

Dr. Jill Johnson, Director
TV Camera and Professional Inst.
25 Fount Ave.
Hollywood, CA   90027

Instead of giving the names and addresses of their references, some people write *References available upon request.* This means that if the reader of the résumé is interested in knowing more about this person, the applicant will supply the names, addresses, and possibly telephone numbers of references. Either approach is acceptable, but if someone is really interested in finding out more about you, it saves time to have the complete information on your résumé. Otherwise, the employer first has to contact you to get the names of your references. If you cannot be easily contacted, your résumé may be put on the bottom of the pile.

There are four golden rules for references:

a. Always get permission from people before you use their names. How embarrassing if they are contacted by a potential employer and they say they don't give references, or the employer is unable to get in touch with them because they're sick or out of town, or they've moved.

b. Be sure to get the correct spelling of the references' names as well as their correct titles (Director, Chairperson, Instructor, Foreman, etc.).

c. Make sure you have the correct address, zip code, and/or telephone number for each reference.

d. Don't use a relative as a reference.

8. After you've handwritten a practice copy of your résumé and have checked it for accuracy of names, addresses, dates, and other details, type a practice copy on a typewriter or word processor. Figure out how to space the information so your résumé will be centered on the page, attractive, and easy to read. Your résumé should not be longer than one page, especially at the beginning of your career. Type a final copy and proofread it again. Then have several photocopies made so you can apply for as many jobs as you want to without having to retype your résumé each time. You can make your résumé look even more professional by having it typeset and printed on high-quality paper at a print shop.

 Practice

Now it's your turn.

TASK: to write a résumé

SITUATION: You want to find a new job, so you need to create a résumé. Write a résumé that will tell potential employers about your work experience, education, and any special skills you have.

UNIT
FOUR

ACADEMICS

CHAPTER 13
Making an Outline

Are you an organized person? Do you plan the night before what you are going to wear the next day? Do you make shopping lists? Do you schedule when you're going to do your homework or certain household tasks? Organized people get more done in less time. It's especially helpful to be organized when you have a paper to write. Knowing how to outline will help you see the benefits of (1) organizing your thoughts on paper, and (2) being able to rearrange your ideas quickly and easily.

 Rationale

An outline determines the shape or form of an essay, just as our skeletons determine the shape of our bodies. The amount and quality of the flesh on our skeletal frames affects the appearance of the final product, us. The amount of work we put into the "fleshing out" of an outline affects the quantity and quality of the final product, the essay. In both cases, it's important to begin with a good basic structure.

An outline is useful for any type of writing, because it helps to organize one's thoughts in a logical or sequential order. In this chapter, we will focus on making an outline for an autobiography. However, the same procedure may be followed to make an outline for any type of writing.

 Materials Needed

paper, pen or pencil

Skills Involved
demonstrating knowledge of alphabet and number sequence, using parallel construction, organizing thoughts

⯈⯈ **Important Vocabulary**

autobiography a history of a person's life written by that person

capital letters letters taking the form *A, B, C,* and so forth

essay here, a relatively short piece of writing, usually on one subject

extracurricular activities here, activities such as clubs and sports that students participate in outside of regular school hours

flesh the skin that covers our bones

flesh out to develop or add to

hobbies the things a person does for fun

logical order an order that makes sense. (If you are writing your autobiography, a *logical order* would be to start with your birth and continue through your lifetime to the present. At the end you might discuss the future.)

lowercase letters letters taking the form *a, b, c,* and so forth

parallel construction using the same grammatical form to express all items in a list or two or more items being compared. *(She likes skating, reading, and cooking* shows parallel construction, while *She likes skating, reading, and to cook* does not.)

rearrange put in a different order

uppercase letters capital letters

Examples

A. Outline for Autobiography of Juan Mendoza

I. Birth
   A. Where
   B. When
II. Early years
   A. School
   B. Friends
   C. Moves
      1. Venezuela
      2. Brooklyn
III. Teen years
   A. School
      1. Subjects
      2. Extracurricular activities
         a. Spanish club
         b. Student council
   B. Hobbies
      1. Guitar
      2. Band
      3. Soccer
   C. Part-time job
IV. Plans for future
   A. College
   B. Career
   C. Family

A typical outline for the autobiography of a high school student might look something like Example A (above). Juan Mendoza was born in one country but moved to two other countries when he was six years old, so he has included a section about "moves" in his early years. As a high school student writing his autobiography for a college application, he has included sections about the most important aspects of his high school career and also his plans for the future.

When Juan writes his autobiography, he will look at his outline and know (1) where to begin, and (2) what to include and in what order. He won't have to trust his ideas to memory because his outline tells him what to include in his essay. The opening paragraph for his essay might look something like this:

I was born in Cali, Colombia, on June 7, 1972. I spent my earliest years in Cali and started school there. I still remember my special friends even though my family moved to Venezuela when I was only six. We lived in Venezuela for a few months and then we moved again, this time to Brooklyn, New York. It was very different from Cali...

B. Outline for Autobiography of Kim Chung

I. Birth
II. Early years
   A. Orphanage
      1. Search for parents
      2. Separation from twin sister
   B. Thailand
   C. U.S.A.
III. Teen years
   A. New family
   B. High school
   C. Friends
   D. Job
IV. Present
   A. Family
      1. Husband
      2. Natural children
      3. Adopted children
         a. Korean
         b. Black
   B. Search for twin sister
   C. Career
   D. College
V. Plans for future

Kim Chung is a young mother with two natural children and two adopted children. She takes care of children of working parents in her home, but she really wants to go to college. She'd like to study bookkeeping, accounting, and using a computer. Her autobiography for a college application might start like this:

> I was born in Vietnam, that much I know, but about my birth I don't know much more. I was raised in an orphanage with other children whose parents were missing. The people in charge couldn't find my parents, but worse than that, they separated my twin sister and me and sent her to a different place. I will never stop looking for her.
>
> When I was four years old, I was claimed by my American father and I spent the next six months at a refugee center in Thailand. Finally, when I was almost five years old, I came to the United States.

The fact that Kim has a family of her own now and that she is very sensitive about her own early years will make the fleshing out of number IV in her outline extremely important. This part of her autobiography will help a college admissions committee to see why she has waited until now to pursue college and to plan for the career she has chosen.

▶ Procedure

Below are some simple points to remember when writing an outline:

> The basic structure of an outline is, in sequential order:

a. Roman numerals

b. capital letters indented under Roman numerals

c. Arabic numerals indented a little more

d. lowercase letters indented a little more

> There should never be a *I* without a *II*, never an *A* without a *B*, never a *1* without a *2*, and never an *a* without a *b*.

> You can use as many letters and numbers as you wish.

> Specific information is not usually given in an outline. Save the details for the writing of the essay.

> Use as few words as possible for each point. Remember to use parallel construction.

Sample format for an outline:

I.

   A.

   B.

      1.

      2.

      3.

         a.

         b.

II.

III.

   A.

      1.

      2.

   B.

   C.

      1.

      2.

         a.

         b.

         c.

Whether the topic for your outline is one you have chosen or one you have been assigned, the procedure is the same:

1. Make a list of the main points you want to include. (These are the points that will probably become topic sentences in your essay.) Put them in the order you want to talk about them and number them with Roman numerals (I, II, III, IV, etc.).

For example, if your outline is about winter weather in the United States, you might divide your information something like this:

Winter Weather in the United States
I. North
II. East
III. South
IV. West

2. Go back to each major topic and list under it the most important points you want to make about that topic. Put these points in a logical order and give each one a capital letter.

For example, you could describe the weather in various sections of each large area:

I. North
A. Northeastern states
B. North-central states
C. Northwestern states

3. Under each letter, use Arabic numerals to include more specific details:

```
I. North
   A. Northeastern states
      1. Rainfall
      2. Snowfall
      3. Temperature highs
      4. Temperature lows
```

4. You can include still more information using lowercase letters:

```
I. North
   A. Northeastern states
      1. Rainfall
      2. Snowfall
         a. amount each year
         b. effect on people's lives, jobs, etc.
```

5. After you finish your outline, look at it carefully.

a. Is your information in good sequential order?

b. Did you use parallel construction? (For example, did you use the same part of speech for all the letters under Roman numeral I?)

6. Rearrange your outline until it is just the way you want it. Keep it right in front of you and use it as a guide when you write your essay. Follow its order and remember:

a. Every Roman numeral in your outline should be the beginning of a new paragraph in your essay.

b. Don't use the numbers or letters in your essay; they are just guides for you.

7. Your outline is just for you. Its purpose is to help you include all that you want to say in your paper in a logical, interesting manner.

▶ **Practice**

Now it's your turn.

TASK: to write an outline for an autobiography

SITUATION: You are applying for college or for a job. You have been asked to write an essay telling about yourself, your background, interests, education, plans for the future, and anything else that might help the people who read your autobiography to decide if you are the kind of person they are looking for. Write an outline for your autobiography.

CHAPTER 14
Writing an Autobiography

If you plan to apply to college, you will almost surely have to write an autobiography, a history of your life. Many job applications also ask for a brief life history. When you go for a job interview, the interviewer almost always asks you to "tell me something about yourself."

▷▷ Rationale

College applications often ask for an autobiography so the admissions committee can get a more complete picture of each potential student. Your autobiography does more than tell about your background and your plans for the future. It also shows your organizational and writing skills. Therefore, it's wise to write an outline first, even though the outline will never be sent to the college. (See the previous chapter for how to write an outline.) It's also important to consider who will be reading your autobiography. Knowing who your reading audience will be will help you focus your autobiography on those points you think will interest them the most.

▷▷ Materials Needed

practice paper, pen or pencil, typewriter or word processor, unlined paper or composition paper

▷▷ Skills Involved

organizing material; writing an outline; writing paragraphs in sequential order; using correct spelling, capitalization, and punctuation

Important Vocabulary

autobiography a history of a person's life written by that person

extracurricular activities here, activities such as clubs and sports that students participate in outside of regular school hours

hobbies the things a person does for fun

skill the ability to do something well, usually developed by means of much practice

talent a natural ability; an ability that one is born with

 **Example**

AUTOBIOGRAPHY OF KIM CHUNG

I was born in Vietnam, that much I know, but about my birth I don't know much more. I was raised in an orphanage with other children whose parents were missing. The people in charge couldn't find my parents, but worse than that, they separated my twin sister and me and sent her to a different place. I will never stop looking for her.

When I was four years old, I was claimed by my American father and I spent the next six months at a refugee center in Thailand. Finally, when I was almost five years old, I came to the United States.

At first it was very difficult coming to this strange country. My father and his wife were very kind to me. Suddenly I had two brothers, Jerry and Johnnie. I was very nervous because I didn't look like anybody else in my family.

When I started school, there were many children from other countries and we all started to learn more about our new country, its culture, and its language. Everyone was very kind to me. My father's wife asked me to call her "Mom" the way my brothers did.

By the time I got to high school, I guess I was as American as I could be. I wore blue jeans and went to football games and had a part-time job at Burger King. My friends were Americans and Vietnamese and we all "hung out" together.

In my senior year of high school I met another Vietnamese whose story was similar to mine. He came to the United States when he was nine years old. He had many relatives here. He was working in his uncle's fruit and vegetable business when I met him. We were married six months after I graduated from high school.

Today, my husband, Lom, and I have two natural children. We have also adopted a Korean child and an American black child. We want to give as much love to as many children as we can in gratitude for our own good fortune.

I will search for my twin sister until I find her or have proof that she is no longer with us. My husband and I have worked very hard to make a good life for our children. He works many hours a day in our store. I take care of children of working parents in our home. Now I would like to go to college to learn how to run our business more efficiently so my husband wouldn't have to work so many hours. I want to study bookkeeping, accounting, and using a computer.

Procedure

1. First make an outline for your autobiography. See the previous chapter on how to write an outline.

2. If you are writing your autobiography as part of an application, be sure to follow any directions regarding content or format. Write or type a practice copy of your autobiography before you put it on the application form.

3. Begin with your beginnings, but unless there are very unusual circumstances, keep this section brief. Readers of applications have hundreds, sometimes thousands, of autobiographies to read. They are not interested in autobiographies that begin, "I was born at the stroke of midnight in the midst of a snowstorm," unless that snowstorm was of some special significance.

4. Go through your early years, noting anything particularly important or significant but keeping in mind that this part, too, should usually be brief.

5. If the autobiography is for a college application, the section that deals with your present activities and with your future plans will be most important to the college admissions board. Therefore, this section should be the longest and the most detailed. Include information about your hobbies, special skills and talents, and/or part-time jobs. If you are in high school, write about *why* you are taking certain courses, what extracurricular activities you're involved in, and any honors or awards you've received. Be sure to end with a paragraph about your plans for the future. If you are attending a community college or are working and not attending school at the time, tell something about your courses, the nature of your work, and your hobbies or other activities, as well as your plans for the future.

If your autobiography is for a job application or some other purpose, focus on the parts of your life that will be most interesting to the reader and tell the most about the kind of person you are.

6. Proofread your practice copy to correct any spelling or punctuation errors. Rewrite any sentences you think you can improve. Then write or type your final copy.

7. Proofread your final copy and correct any errors. Because your autobiography is an introduction to you, be sure to take pride in its appearance.

▶ Practice

Now it's your turn.

TASK: to write an autobiography. (If you've already written an outline for an autobiography for the previous chapter, work from that outline. Otherwise, see pages 114–124 for help in creating an outline before you begin writing your autobiography.)

SITUATION: You are filling out an application that calls for an autobiography. You may either type your autobiography or write it by hand.

CHAPTER 15
Writing an Essay

The word *essay* has many meanings. Two of the most important definitions for *essay* as the word is used in school are as follows:

1. a one-paragraph or longer written answer to a test question

2. several paragraphs written about a subject, in which the writer expresses his or her opinions or tries to make certain points, using details or facts to support each idea or opinion. A book report is one kind of essay. (See pages 140–141 for an example of this kind of essay.) A written review of a movie or TV program is also an essay.

 Rationale

Knowing how to write an essay can open a variety of careers to you as a writer/columnist or reviewer for newspapers, magazines, radio, and/or television, to name just one type of professional opportunity. Educationally, the ability to write good essay answers to test questions is becoming more and more important as educators and members of the business community recognize the need for people to be able to express themselves in an intelligent, organized fashion. Other chapters in this book deal with various forms of essay writing. (See "Writing an Autobiography" and "Writing a Book Report.") This section focuses on essay answers to test questions.

Materials Needed

practice paper, pencil; pen and composition paper, or typewriter/word processor and unlined paper

Skills Involved

organizing ideas and information; supplying specific details or facts to support ideas and information; writing sentences and paragraphs (writing a topic sentence with supporting details in following sentences); using correct spelling, punctuation, and capitalization

 ## Important Vocabulary

columnist a person who writes essays on topics of his or her choice for a newspaper or magazine

concluding ending; the concluding sentence is the last sentence

mass media methods of communication such as radio, television, newspapers, and magazines that are designed to reach many, many people at once

personnel the people who work for an organization

reviewer a person who gives his or her opinion (orally or in writing) on a recent book, play, musical, radio or television show, or other event for one of the mass media

supporting details specific facts or information that can be used to prove what you're saying is true

topic sentence a sentence that states the main idea of a paragraph, often the first sentence

Example

Test question:

How can schools get parents to work more closely with them in the education of their children?

Essay answer:

One thing school personnel have to realize is that there may be many reasons why parents don't come to school. The fact that they don't come to school doesn't necessarily mean they don't care about their children or they aren't helping their children at home. Some parents may not come to school to talk to teachers because they work during school hours. Parents who have come here from other countries may not come to school because they don't speak English or they are embarrassed by their accents and their limited English. Other parents may not come to school because they don't have anyone to take care of their babies. Many parents from other countries think the schools know what is best for their children and believe they are not supposed to come to school to ask questions. Questioning their children's teachers is not something they would do in their native countries. They think of school personnel as professionals who know their jobs and who shouldn't be bothered by parents, or who might even be angry or insulted if parents dared to question them.

There are ways for schools to help parents to work more closely with them in the education of their children. Schools can send home bilingual messages in English and in the parents' native language announcing meetings, suggesting ways of helping their children, giving parents

topic sentence

supporting details

topic sentence

supporting details

information they should have, and asking parents if they have any questions. Schools can also arrange meetings be-tween parents and teachers at times that are convenient for both groups, providing some kind of volunteer baby-sitting service in the school so parents with younger children can attend. Another thing schools can do is to have teachers visit groups of parents in one parent's home, to discuss problems and solutions on the parents' home ground. That would probably make the parents feel more comfortable. It would take a lot of planning, but it would be good because it would also give teachers and other school personnel who attend a chance to see where and how their students live. School personnel would become better educated about their students and this would help them in their future planning.

concluding sentence

 Procedure

When writing an essay answer to a test question, you should:

1. Study ahead of time for the test.

2. Read the test question carefully and, on a separate piece of paper, write down in abbreviated form all the relevant information that comes to your mind. Even if this is a timed test, you'll still have time to organize and complete your essay because your notes are not in complete sentences; they are more like an outline of what you want to remember to include in your answer.

For example, if the question is in history and you are asked how various wars affected United States foreign policy, you'll first want to remember as many wars as possible that you studied in class. You might write down their names as they come into your head:

Fr-Ind
1812
Rev
Civil
W W 1
W W 2
Korean
Vietnam
Span-Amer

(The abbreviations refer to the French and Indian War, the Revolutionary War, World Wars 1 and 2, and the Spanish-American War.)

Then you can refer to this list, put the wars in the correct chronological order (the order in which they occurred), and write about how each one affected United States foreign policy. This method is easier than having to stop and think after you write about each war, and it reduces your chances of leaving out one or two.

3. After you write your topic sentence for each paragraph, be sure to give as many reasons or facts as you can to support what you've written. See the topic sentences and supporting details in the example on pages 133–134.

4. At the end of your essay, write a concluding sentence to summarize what you've said; for example, *This shows how the United States' foreign policy has been affected by various wars the country has been involved in.*

5. Proofread, if you have time. Correct and rewrite whatever you feel needs improving. Be sure you have proved your points.

 Practice

Now it's your turn.

TASK: to write an essay answer to a test question

SITUATION: You are taking a test and must answer this question:

How can an understanding of various cultures help us in our personal and professional lives? Use your own experience and the experiences of people you know or have read about to prove your points.

CHAPTER 16
Writing a Book Report

Have you ever heard or read something about a book that made you really want to read that book? Or have you ever read a book you couldn't wait to tell someone else about because you enjoyed it so much or because you were so disappointed in it?

Newspapers and magazines often publish book reviews that make people feel they must get a certain book immediately or decide this is one book they're really not interested in reading. Television news programs often talk about new books, movies, or plays people should know about. The reviewers tell why they liked or didn't like each play, movie, or book and then give some examples to prove their points. In the media, these are called *reviews*. In school, they're usually called *reports*. This chapter is about writing one kind of report—a book report.

 Rationale

There are many reasons for writing a book report. A major reason is to share something about a book with other people so they can decide if they would like to read the book. Writing book reports improves our organizational and writing skills, helps us recognize the most important points an author is making, and gives us an opportunity to express our opinions. It may even lead to a career as a reviewer for a newspaper, a magazine, or a radio or television station.

 Materials Needed

pen, practice paper, composition paper or typewriter/word processor and unlined paper

⨠ Skills Involved

reading comprehension; organizing thoughts; evaluating what you've read; expressing opinion; offering supporting details; summarizing; using correct spelling, capitalization, and punctuation

⨠ Important Vocabulary

accomplishments things a person has done

autobiography a history of a person's life written by that person

biography a history of a person's life written by someone else

conclusion a final decision, based on certain facts and feelings

evaluating deciding for yourself the value or quality of something

expressing opinion telling how you feel about something

expressions words and phrases used for saying something

fiction literature that is not true

gestures facial or body movements used for communication

nonfiction literature that is true

parentheses punctuation marks ( ) used to show that certain information is interesting or useful but not absolutely necessary

plot the plan for a story; the events that take place in a story

summarizing telling in a few words or sentences the main ideas of a larger piece of writing

supporting details specific facts or information that can be used to prove what you're saying is true

theme the topic or subject of a story

Example

Review of
Everyday Japanese by Edward Schwarz and Reiko Ezawa

topic
sentence

Everyday Japanese, A Basic Introduction to the Japanese Language and Culture is divided into three parts, each of which gives the reader a clearer picture of life in modern Japan. Part One, "Getting Around in Japan," gives general conversation and introductions and teaches the non-Japanese-speaking person how to buy a ticket at the train

specific
details

station, take a taxi, check in and out of a hotel, make appointments, shop, and be understood at the doctor's office, the drugstore, the post office, and so forth. All the "Useful Expressions" are written both in the Roman alphabet and in Japanese, with the English translation in parentheses. The pronunciation of the letters in Japanese and the symbols used are explained in the introduction. It is very important that the reader begin Everyday Japanese by reading all the material before Part One.

Part Two, "Only in Japan," teaches the reader important expressions and correct behavior at a tea ceremony, theater and sporting events, temples and shrines, and in a Japanese house. It also teaches about Japanese holidays and festivals, clothing, and the Japanese bath. Students not only learn the appropriate words, phrases, and behavior for various places and occasions, they also learn the history or reasons behind each activity and behavior. They learn the language and the culture, as the book says in its title.

Part Three of the book is about "Living in Japan" and is very important for people planning to move there from another country. It has useful expressions in sections on the immigration office, buying or renting a house or an apartment, automobiles, gestures, and counting in Japanese.

Every section of <u>Everyday Japanese</u> has an illustration and a vocabulary list of twenty words. There are useful expressions and dialogues to practice, and notes that tell about the culture and why things are done a certain way.

I liked this book because I'm interested in learning the Japanese language and also because I like to learn about other cultures. I found it very interesting that <u>karate</u> means "empty hand" and that a karate expert can break bricks and piles of wood with his bare hand. I also found it interesting that the Japanese take off their shoes before entering a house. The Japanese can fold up their beds, called <u>futons</u>, and put them away when they get up in the morning. The most fascinating thing to me was that before the Japanese take a bath, they wash themselves <u>outside</u> the tub. The tub is kept clean and can be used more than once before the water is changed.

specific
details

I would recommend this book to anyone who wants to learn something about Japanese culture. People who would like to learn some useful Japanese expressions for traveling or living in Japan would also find <u>Everyday Japanese</u> helpful.

conclusion

Myra Androyan

▶ **Procedure**

If your teacher has given you a list of questions to answer about the book, or has given you specific directions for how the report is to be written, be sure to follow those directions carefully. Usually you will be asked to write a summary of the book and to tell why you did or didn't like it. It is always best to write a practice copy first so you can correct your mistakes and rewrite any sentences you don't like. You can also take out anything you decide is not necessary and check to make sure that you have given examples to support your opinions. Here are some general guidelines for writing a book report:

1. Give the title and author of the book. It's often a good idea to include the name of the publisher (the company that printed the book) and the year it was published, too.

2. Begin by telling something about the book.

a. Is it fiction or nonfiction?

b. Is it divided in a way that is important for the reader to know?

3. If the book is fiction:

a. Tell something about the characters and how they are involved in the story. Don't give away the plot or the ending, but try to make the reader want to read the book by describing something you found really exciting or fascinating. This is called "creating suspense," making the reader wonder what happens next. If no such excitement occurred for you, you can say this too, again using examples to show why the author didn't accomplish his or her purpose.

b. Tell whether the characters and the plot were believable. Use examples to explain why or why not.

c. Tell something about what you liked and/or didn't like about this book. What made you choose it?

4. If the book is nonfiction:

a. Tell what kind of book it is (autobiography, biography, history book, travel book, etc.).

b. If it's an autobiography or a biography, explain what made this person worthy of having a book written about him or her. Name some of the person's specific accomplishments. Tell how you felt about this person when you finished reading the book. Why did you feel this way? Be very specific, giving details from the book to illustrate (explain) your points.

c. If the book you read was a history book, tell something about the period of time covered and why a book was written about this time. Describe your reactions to this time and the events that took place. Would you like to have lived at that time? Why or why not? Be very specific.

d. If the book you read was a travel book, tell something about the places written about in the book. Explain why the author wrote about those particular places. Now that you've read the book, tell why you would or wouldn't want to visit or live in those places. Be very specific, giving examples or details from the book to support your opinions.

e. Explain what you liked and/or didn't like about the book. What made you choose it?

5. Avoid overusing the word *interesting* when you tell how you feel about a book. This word is used so much it has lost its meaning. If you found the book exciting, give an example of *what* was exciting. If it was boring, show *why*, with an example. A good book report is a combination of "tell" and "show." You want the readers of your book report to believe what you're saying, so after you *tell* what you think and how you feel, *show* why you feel this way by giving some specific details or facts.

6. End your report by telling why you would or would not recommend this book to others. Be very specific about your reasons.

▶ Practice

Now it's your turn.

TASK: to write a book report

SITUATION: You have been assigned to write a book report. Choose a book you have read recently and write a report about the book.

CHAPTER 17
Taking Notes from a Lecture

Whether you're in school or not, you probably find yourself attending a lecture, speech, meeting, debate, or class at least occasionally. Often, you want to remember the speaker's most important points so you can study for a future exam, use the information in an essay or research paper, ask questions or challenge a point, or have a record of what was said for use in a future meeting or debate. One way to remember the most important points of any talk is to take notes on what the speaker says.

▷▷ Rationale

It isn't easy to take notes when someone is speaking, because you usually can't go back and have things repeated and because you have to keep listening to the next thing being said while you're writing down what you just heard. For these reasons, some people take tape recorders to classes or lectures so they can record what is being said, but this is not always a good idea. Sometimes the sound is not good and you can't understand what is on the tape afterward, or there are other noises on the tape that make it hard to listen to. Also, you get a lot of information you may not want or need, and you have to spend time listening to the whole talk again as you pick out the material you want. Finally, relying on a tape recorder can make you lazy and leave you with a big problem if the machine breaks or isn't available. It's important to develop your listening and concentration skills, along with your note-taking skills.

▷▷ Materials Needed
notebook, pens or pencils

Skills Involved

listening comprehension, concentrating, recognizing key thoughts, condensing, being able to listen and write at the same time

 Important Vocabulary

abbreviation a shortened form of a word; for example, *Dr.* for *doctor, appt.* for *appointment*

concentrating keeping your mind on the subject you are listening to or reading about

debate a discussion between two or more people who don't agree on a subject. Each person tries to prove that his or her opinion is correct.

lazy not wanting to work

lecture a talk given by a professor or other authority on a subject

relying depending

taking notes writing down in abbreviated form what you want to remember from something you're reading or hearing

tape recorder a small machine that can record sound on a special kind of tape and can play that sound back later

 Example

Look at this short lecture and pretend you are listening to it. Remember, it's much easier to read this than to listen to it, so read it *only one time* because you would be hearing it only one time.

TABLE MANNERS, AMERICAN STYLE

There are several ways in which American dining customs differ from those elsewhere. An invited dinner guest is expected to arrive at the specified time, contrary to the customs in some countries. The use of the knife and fork is often different. The fork is used mostly in the right hand. It gathers the food without help from the knife, which is generally used only to cut meat and potatoes, and is to the right of the plate when not in use. And while in many places the napkin (cloth or paper used to clean the lips and hands at the table) is put around the neck, here it is put on the lap (the top part of the legs of a seated person). Finally, Americans tend to eat foods with their fingers. At informal dinners and picnics, chicken, corn-on-the-cob, pizza, and tortillas (a Mexican food) are eaten without utensils (knives, forks, and spoons).[1]

Your notes from the lecture might look like this:

Amer. Table Manners - 3/1 - Stacia St. Claire

Amer. din. cust. diff. from other places. (1) Guests arr. on time. (2) Fork mostly in rt. hand. (3) Don't use knife to help. (4) Knife for cut. meat, pot. (5) Knife to rt. of plate when not using. (6) Napkin on lap. (7) Some food eaten w/ fingers, espec. at picnics, etc.

Naturally, you would use your own form of shorthand and abbreviations, but see if you can make sense out of these notes since you have read the actual lecture. The first information given is the subject of the talk (American table manners), the date of the lecture (March 1), and the name of the speaker. Notice the period (.) at the end of each abbreviation.

---

[1] Jann Huizenga, *Looking at American Food* (Lincolnwood, IL: National Textbook Co., 1987) 30.

Procedure

1. Have your notebook and pen or pencil ready.

2. Before the speaker begins, write the date and title or subject of the lecture or class. If the person giving the lecture is not your regular teacher, you might want to write the speaker's name, too.

3. Listen for the main idea and examples to prove it. Write these down as you hear them.

4. Abbreviate words and use your own shorthand. You don't have to number your notes, but you may do so if it will help to organize them. They are numbered in the example on page 147 because each numbered statement represents an example of the main idea that "American dining customs differ from those in other places."

5. Write only the most important facts.

It is very good practice to listen to newscasts on the radio and take notes from them. Since the same news is often broadcast several times a day, you can check your notes at different times to see how complete and accurate they are.

Practice

Now it's your turn.

TASK: to take notes from a lecture

SITUATION: You are attending a lecture on test-taking. Listen to the lecture* and take notes on the most important points. Remember, you will hear the lecture only once and at a normal speaking rate, so concentrate on what is being said as you write.

---

*Your teacher will read or play the lecture for you. However, the text of the lecture is printed in Appendix B. If you are studying independently, try to find someone to read it to you so you can practice taking notes from a listening situation. If there is no one to read the conversation to you, look at the text and take notes from it, remembering that this is not quite the same as hearing the words without being able to see them or have them repeated.

CHAPTER 18
Taking Notes from a Reading

When you read a book, article, or other piece of writing, you often want to remember the main points of what you've read. One way to do this is by taking notes as you read. Later, when you want to remember what the book or article was about, you can look at your notes instead of reading the whole thing again.

 Rationale

If you're in school, it's a good idea to take notes whenever you read an assignment from a textbook or other source. Then you can use your notes to study before a test or final exam. Even if you're not in school, you probably read books or articles related to your work, hobbies, or other interests. Taking notes as you read gives you a record of what you have read that you can look at any time.

 Materials Needed

textbook or other reading material, pen or pencil, notebook or index cards (3″ × 5″ or larger)

 Skills Involved

reading comprehension; using abbreviations; recognizing topic sentences, key words, and key phrases; summarizing; recognizing what's important for a particular situation (for example, what material you need to study for a particular exam or what facts you need to prove a certain point)

Important Vocabulary

abbreviation a shortened form of a word; for example, *Dr.* for *doctor, appt.* for *appointment*

key words most important words

points ideas you want people to know, think about, and/or understand

shorthand a form of writing that uses special signs, letters, and abbreviations to make note-taking easier and faster (*&* for *and* and *w* for *with* are forms of shorthand.)

single only one

source a person, place, or object that contains information

summarize tell in a few words or sentences the main ideas of a larger piece of writing

taking notes writing down in abbreviated form what you want to remember from something you're reading or hearing

topic sentence a sentence that states the main idea of a paragraph, often the first (or sometimes the last) sentence

Example

Read this information on "Alphabetical Order," then look at the notes taken from it.

ALPHABETICAL ORDER[1]

There are twenty-six letters in the English alphabet. Every English student should know the alphabet. The letters are abcdefghijklmnopqrstuvwxyz. It is important to know the order of the alphabet. It is often used to organize books and parts of books. It helps you find words in a dictionary, for example. It helps you find which book to use in an encyclopedia of many books.

Sometimes alphabetical order uses only the letters, like this: A–E; F–I; J–L; M–O; P–S; T–Z. Sometimes, especially in a library, alphabetical order is by the first letter of names or words. . . .

---

[1]Margaret Martin Maggs, *English Across the Curriculum 2* (Lincolnwood, IL: National Textbook Co., 1983) 1–3.

In alphabetical order, sometimes there are two words that begin with the same letter. An example of this is **and** and **apple.** What do you do then? You use the second letter to help you alphabetize (put in alphabetical order). In the word **and** the second letter is N. In the word **apple** the second letter is P. N is before P in the alphabet. The word **and** is before **apple** in alphabetical order.

Notes from a single source can be put either in a notebook or on index cards. Whichever you use, be sure to include the necessary information about the source. The notes shown below are in a notebook. For longer reports, index cards are easier to use, as you will see in the next chapter.

source {

English Across the Curriculum 2
Margaret Martin Maggs
National Textbook Co., Lincolnwood, IL 1983
pages 1-3

26 letters in Eng. alphabet. All Eng. students should know alpha. Imp. know order of alpha. Used to organize books, dict., encycl. Sometimes only lttrs used on bks. When 1st let. of wds same, wds alpha. by 2nd let., e. g., and, apple.

Cover the reading and look only at the notes. Can you make any sense out of them? It will be easier to read your own notes, of course, because you will have your own way of abbreviating. Without looking at the original reading, see if you can write a few sentences just from the notes. When you're finished, look at the reading again. Did you get the main idea? What kind of notes would you have taken?

▶ Procedure

1. Look at the end of the chapter or section you are preparing to read. Are there questions to be answered? These questions are often the key to the main points of the reading. *Read the questions first.* Then, when you read the chapter, the most important points will "jump out" at you. You'll be able to answer the questions and you'll know what the author considers most important. These are the points you'll especially want to take notes on.

2. Use your own shorthand and abbreviations to take notes. For example, don't write words like *a, and,* or *the.* Abbreviate words like *information (info.), association (assoc.), with (w),* and *including (incl.).* One easy way to abbreviate is to leave out the vowels (*a, e, i, o, u*) in some words; for example, *signed* becomes *sgnd.* The important thing is to use abbreviations that you are comfortable with and that you will remember the meaning of when you need to read your notes again at a later date.

3. Don't use complete sentences in your notes. If a sentence in the article reads,

> The Declaration of Independence of the United States of America was signed by many important people, including Thomas Jefferson, John Hancock, and Benjamin Franklin.

your notes might read,

> *Dec. of Ind. sgnd by mny imp. ppl, incl. T. Jefferson, J. Hancock, B. Franklin.*

If you don't think you'll remember the men's first names, you might abbreviate Jefferson's as *Thom.* and Franklin's as *Ben* or *Benj.*

4. Keep your notes in a notebook and write them in ink so they'll be easy to read when you want to study from them at a future date.

5. It's always a good idea to mark down the name of the book and the pages you took your notes from. You may also want to list the chapter number and/or title so you can turn back to it quickly when you need to.

6. When you finish taking notes, always read them over to be sure they make sense to you. If you don't understand something now, it's going to be a lot harder to understand a week or a month from now. Go back to the reading and see what you meant to write. Then fix your notes while it's easy to do so.

▶ **Practice**

Now it's your turn.

TASK: to take notes from a reading

SITUATION: You have been assigned to read this passage from *The Birthday of the United States* by Gustavo Maja (Austin, Texas: Voluntad Publishers, 1979).

Countries have birthdays, just as you and I do.
And every year the United States has a giant birthday party.
The United States' birthday is the 4th of July.
This is the story of the birth of the United States.

Many years ago, the American states were not united. They were part of a country called Great Britain. All the laws were made far away by King George the Third. King George made everyone pay him a lot of money in taxes. The people in the American colonies did not like the laws. Samuel Adams and Tom Paine loved America. They wanted America to be free to make its own laws. They spoke to many Americans about their ideas. They wanted America to be a new country.

King George sent soldiers to make the ideas stop. Instead there was a war. Paul Revere rode his horse all one night to warn people that the soldiers were on their way. They quickly got up and armed themselves to fight for their freedom.

The soldiers sent by King George wore beautiful uniforms. These British soldiers came from faraway Great Britain to fight against the American colonies and make them obey King George's laws.

The American patriots were not soldiers. They did not wear uniforms, but they were very brave people. They fought against the soldiers so the colonies could be free states. They fought for the right to unite and form a new nation.

The war for independence was long and very hard. Some of the patriots gathered together; their meeting was called a congress. Thomas Jefferson wrote a letter—a Declaration of Independence—and they all signed it. Some of the signers were Benjamin Franklin, Samuel Adams, and John Hancock.

The Declaration listed all the problems that King George had caused the people in the colonies. It also said that everyone should have a chance to give an opinion. That idea is called democracy. The Declaration of

Independence was signed on the 4th of July more than two hundred years ago.

The war was not over yet, but that letter was the birth of the United States of America. It was born during a war, but the war was won later. And every year that birthday is celebrated by Americans living all over the world. It is a day of great joy. Flags can be seen everywhere.

The flag now has fifty stars—one for each free state. And it has thirteen stripes—one for each of the colonies that fought the war for independence.

The 4th of July is the biggest national holiday. There are parades, picnics, music, and parties everywhere. Stores close, and people go camping and visit their friends. In the evening there are fireworks for everyone to enjoy. It is the biggest birthday party of the year. It is a celebration of the signing of the Declaration of Independence on the 4th of July many years ago. It is the birthday of the United States of America.

Questions:

1. When is the United States' birthday?

2. What is the Declaration of Independence?

3. Who are some of the men who signed the Declaration?

4. Who was Paul Revere?

5. What are "patriots"?

6. Who was king of Great Britain during the time of the war?

Read your notes over. Write a paragraph or two from your notes. Check what you've written against the original reading. How accurate and complete are your notes?

Did you remember to look for questions at the end before you began your reading? Answer the questions now. Are they easy to answer from your notes? If not, go back through the reading and see what important points you missed.

CHAPTER 19
Taking Notes from Multiple Sources

When you read more than one book or talk to more than one person about a particular topic, it's easy to forget later where you read or heard a certain piece of information. If you plan to write a paper or give a speech on that topic, it's important to know where you got every piece of information you use. Taking notes as you read or listen will give you a record of all your information and where it came from.

 ## Rationale

During the course of your education, you will probably have to write more than one term paper or research paper. These kinds of papers usually require you to use information from many different sources. When you are collecting facts for a report or presentation of any kind, it's hard to rely on memory alone. Therefore, it's important to learn good note-taking skills.

 ## Materials Needed

pens or pencils, reading materials, index cards (3″ × 5″ or larger)

 ## Skills Involved

reading comprehension; using abbreviations; recognizing topic sentences, key words, and key phrases; summarizing; recognizing what you need to know for a particular situation (for example, what material you need to study for a particular exam or what facts you need to prove a certain point)

Important Vocabulary

abbreviation a shortened form of a word; for example, *Dr.* for *doctor, appt.* for *appointment*

author writer

bibliography a list of sources appearing at the end of a book, article, research paper, or other reading. It tells the title, author, publisher, publication date, and pages for each source.

footnoting making a note at the bottom of a page to tell where you got a certain piece of information

index cards small white cards, usually lined on one side and unlined on the other. The most common size is $3'' \times 5''$ (three inches by five inches).

key words most important words

multiple many; more than one

points ideas you want people to know, understand, and/or think about

quote one person's words repeated exactly in a piece of writing or speech by another person. Whenever you use a quote in a paper, you must use quotation marks (") around the exact words that you are quoting. You must also give credit to the person you are quoting, usually in a footnote

research searching (looking) for and reading information from many sources about a particular topic

research paper a paper of several pages that usually deals with one subject in depth and is based on information learned through research

shorthand a form of writing that uses special letters, signs, and abbreviations to make note-taking easier and faster (& for *and* and *w* for *with* are forms of shorthand.)

source a person, place, or object that contains information

summarize tell in a few words or sentences the main ideas of a larger piece of writing

taking notes writing down in abbreviated form what you want to remember from something you're reading or hearing

term paper a paper on a particular subject, usually due near the end of a school term. A term paper usually requires research and has footnotes and a bibliography.

title the name of a book, speech, play, or other work

topic sentence a sentence that states the main idea of a paragraph, often the first (or sometimes the last) sentence of the paragraph

Example

You are preparing to write a term paper about aspects of Japanese culture an American needs to know before visiting or moving to Japan. You go to the library and look in the card catalog or on-line catalog for information on this subject. You find five books that contain material on the subject, so you make a "bibliography card" for each one, giving each source its own number:

①

Everyday Japanese
Edward A. Schwartz and Reiko Ezawa
Passport Books, Lincolnwood, Illinois, 1985
224 pgs.

②

Japan Today!
Theodore F. Welch and Hiroki Kato
Passport Books, Lincolnwood, Illinois, 1989
128 pgs.

(3)

Japanese Etiquette and Ethics in Business
Boye De Mente
Passport Books, Lincolnwood, Illinois, 1987
192 pgs.

(4)

The Japanese Influence on America
Boye De Mente
Passport Books, Lincolnwood, Illinois, 1989
192 pgs.

(5)

How to Do Business with the Japanese
Boye De Mente
Passport Books, Lincolnwood, Illinois, 1987
256 pgs.

Then you take notes from each book as you read it, writing just one or two points on each card and making sure to put the source number (from the bibliography card) and the appropriate page number(s) at the top of each card:

①   p. 62

Tel. booths diff. colrs. fr. diff. calls: blue = for any dist.; tall red = long dist.; short red = locl.; yellow = espec. good for long dist.

①   p. 96

tea cer. very spec. Hosts and guests have spec. formal roles; takes time to learn.

① pp. 128-129

Shinto native religion; means "way of the gods"; no one great fig. of worship; collection of beliefs & ideas abt. proper way of behavior.

① pp. 136-139

Holidays: Respect for the Aged Day; Adults' Day; Children's Day; Culture Day; Labor Thanksgiving Day; Dolls' Festival; Girls' Festival; Boys' Fest.; Fest. of the Weaver; a day of the children of 3, 5, 7 (Girls 3 & 7, boys 5 taken to shrines. Everyone prays for their continued health.)

① p. 156

Always leave shoes outside. No shoes in Jap. house. No slippers in tatami room. (Tatami mats typ. floor.) Guest of honor given special seat in front of takonoma or alcove.

Visa needed. Visitors must carry passports all time. 16 diff. statuses for vsit. Jap. Let. of guarantee req. by foreigners who want to stay long time. Should be prepared by Jap. ind. or organ. who will promise to assist foreigner if has financial or other prob. Students need special visa to prove actively engaged in study.

Jap. room size measured by # of tatami mats in them.

Flush toilets not taken for granted when buying or renting house.

①   p. 166

"Thank you" money paid to landlord non-refund. Very expensive move to Jap. 1 or 2 mos. rent + security dep. + "thank you" money when move in.

---

②   p. 11

Communal baths. Wash first. One is clean before entering bathtub in hotel or home.

---

②   p. 28

Educ. 6-3-3-4 system: 6 yrs. elem.; 3 yrs. mid. sch.; 3 hgh sch.; 4 col. 1st 9 yrs. free & compulsory. Juku, or supp. schools, help to prepare for col. entr. tests.

③ p. 22

Vertical society - superior/subordinate relationships, ranking.

③ p. 37

"Wa" or "circle" - mutual trust bet. manager & labor. Loyalty, mutual respons., job security, no competitive pressure; collective resp. for decisions & results. No fool. arnd in workplace.

③ p. 44

Westerners easy to get to know early but not deeply. Jap. take longer to know but are more vulnerable.

③   p. 27

Name cards tell rank. Bilingual name
cards handed Jap. side up, presented
with both hands and light bow.
Can see person's rank on card, estab.
vertic. order, language to be used.
Really a ceremony.

④   p. 157

Still a lot of arranged marriages in
Jap. Mar. services provided by many
large cos. Jap. males at 30 pressured by
large cos. to marry. Serious handicap
to promotion if not married.

④   p. 161

School 240 days of yr. Amer. Occup. in
1945 elim. "shushin" or "moral educ."
Jap. believe "success in life dtermined
by academic achievement and respect
for rights of others."

④   p. 139

Shoes not worn inside for sanitary reas. Would bring dust and dirt & get on mats. Spec. alcove where shoes kept when not used.

---

④   p. 141

Sleep on futons. Roll up & put away when fin. sleep.

---

④   pp. 148-149

Dining cust.: (a) rest. give wet cloths when sit down; hot in winter, cold in sum. (b) Jap. tip in advance. Expect good service. Tips not to employees but to rest. or hotel to defray cost of benefits to employees. (c) Guests at party expected to be part of entertainment.

⑤   p. 249

No place on Jap. lic. for hair or eye color.

⑤   p. 149

In offices & in homes, where seated spells rank. Nearest door, lowest rank. Farthest from door in office, highest rank.

⑤   p. 239

Amer. wives w/out Jap. lang. find diff. to adjust; husbands entertain, wives traditionally not incl. Very exp. live there. Children have easy access to alcohol.

⑤   p. 248

Very expensive own private car. Have to take many tests before can get lic., incl. mechanics test to demonstrate know. of engine and how to make repairs.

---

⑤   p. 249

To get license in Japan, must:
1) attend govt.-reg. course (abt. 6 wks. & $1500) incl.
    a) 25 hrs. class lect. & 5 hrs. on construction & oper. of veh.
    b) practice dry runs on simulator
    c) take 17 sessions on driving range w instructor
2) get learner's permit so can then
    a) drive on selected roads and streets
    b) have 10 hrs. off-range driv. in designated areas.

---

⑤   p. 249

Drive on left side in Jap.

⑤   p. 255

Jap. mix bus. & pleas. Men away from home a lot. Don't entertain at home as Amer. do.

⑤   p. 257

Psychological problems facing for. - tremend. crowded: narrow, winding sts. w/out sidewalks outside major cities. For. res. in Jap. aware of being outsiders.

⑤   p. 102

Bus. done differently. Jap. sit back and wait; Amer. put all on table, unnerved by "inscrutable Orientals." Jap. shrewd negotiators.

See Appendix C for an example showing how the notes taken from these sources can be combined to make a smooth paper.

 Procedure

1. When you are taking notes from more than one source for a term paper or research paper, it's a good idea to use index cards instead of notebook paper so you can rearrange your information easily before you begin writing the paper.

2. Each time you read from a different source, make a "bibliography card" that tells

a. the name of the book or magazine you are taking the information from,

b. the author(s),

c. the name and city of the publisher,

d. the year of publication, and

e. the pages you read. (If you read the entire book, write the number of pages in the book.)

A bibliography card might look like this:

source number	①
book title	*High School Students in 20th Century U.S. Urban Areas*
author	Maurice H. Pillsbury
publisher, city, state, publication date	Effective Publishers, Paterson, N.H., 1986
pages read (pages in book)	66 pp.

Notice the source number printed and circled at the top of the card. Give every source you use a different number.

3. Take notes as you read each book or article, writing just one or two points on each index card. Put the number of the source you're using (from the bibliography card) and the appropriate page number(s) at the top of each note card:

> ①   p. 72
> Students not allowed to wear
> shorts to school at beginning
> of 20th cent.

4. Write your notes in your own words, using abbreviations to save time. If you *do* copy a sentence or two exactly from the source, be sure to put quotation marks (") around the exact words. Check to make sure you've written the page number where you found the quote at the top of the card. You will need this information when you write your paper.

5. When you have finished your research, find a place where you can lay out all your note cards. Put the cards in groups according to the information written on them; for example, all the cards about American schools in one pile and all the cards about French schools in another pile. Then put the sentences from your cards in an order that makes sense to you. It's easy to arrange and rearrange your ideas and information when you're working with index cards.

6. After you have all your notes in order, you can begin to write your paper. See "Writing a Term/Research Paper," pages 186–191, for how to continue the process.

7. Save your bibliography cards to use in footnoting and making a bibliography. See the next chapter on "Writing a Bibliography."

Practice

Now it's your turn.

TASK: to take notes from several sources for a research paper

SITUATION: You are preparing to write a research paper on holidays in the United States and how they are celebrated. Go to the library and find at least four sources with information on this topic. Take notes from each source.

Now look back at your notes. Did you remember to:

1. make bibliography cards with the titles and other information about your sources?

2. number the bibliography cards and the cards you took notes on so you can match them easily?

3. put the information in your own words, using abbreviations and your own shorthand?

4. write down only information that relates to your subject, "Holidays in the United States and How They Are Celebrated"?

5. write only one or two sentences on each card?

If so, you're ready for the next two chapters of this book!

CHAPTER 20
Writing a Bibliography

Bibliography is a long word, but it has a very simple meaning and purpose. A bibliography is a list of the sources of information a person used to write a term paper, research paper, or essay, or to prepare for a debate on a particular subject. For each source, a bibliography tells (a) the author and title of the material, (b) who published the material, (c) where and when it was published, and sometimes (d) the pages on which the material appears. A bibliography usually appears at the end of a long paper or book.

 Rationale

If you have written a paper that includes information, facts, or opinions taken from various sources, you should include a bibliography so that readers of your paper can go to your sources for a variety of reasons:

1. Your paper may make them want to read more on the subject because they find it so fascinating.

2. They may want to read for themselves exactly what a particular source says to see if you have expressed the information completely and correctly.

3. They may challenge what you have written. If you give them your sources of information, they can see for themselves that you expressed the information correctly.

4. They may want to see how much reading and research you did before writing the paper.

In addition, it's important to give credit to the people whose ideas and information you used. A bibliography is one way to do this.

Materials Needed

bibliography cards listing the author, title, publisher, date and place of publication, and pages for each of your sources (see previous chapter on "Taking Notes from Multiple Sources"); typewriter or word processor; unlined paper; model entries for a bibliography

Skills Involved

gathering information, organizing material, alphabetizing, typing or word processing, proofreading

Important Vocabulary

alphabetizing putting words in alphabetical order (words starting with *a* first, words starting with *b* next, etc.)

bibliography a list of sources appearing at the end of a book, article, research paper, or other reading. It tells the title, author, publisher, publication date, and pages for each source.

challenge question the truth of something

emigration leaving your country to live in another country. (An *emigrant* from one country is an *immigrant* in the country he or she moves to.)

express show feelings or thoughts in words

organize put things in order

publication date for a book, the year it was printed; for a magazine, the date (month/day/year) of the issue

publisher a company that prepares, prints, and sells books, magazines, or other written materials

research searching (looking) for and reading information from many sources about a particular topic

source a person, place, or object that contains information

title the name of a book, speech, play, or other work

 **Example**

BIBLIOGRAPHY

Baron, Bruce, Christine Baron, and Bonnie MacDonald. What Did
You Learn in School Today? New York: Warner Books Inc.,
1983.

The Chicago Manual of Style. 13th ed. Chicago: The University of
Chicago Press, 1982.

Collier, Herbert L. How to Help Your Child Get Better Grades. New
York: Pinnacle Books, 1981.

Glasser, William. Schools without Failure. New York: Harper and
Row, 1969.

Maculaitis, Jean, and Mona Scheraga. The Complete ESL/EFL
Resource Book. Lincolnwood, IL: National Textbook Co.,
1988.

Maggs, Margaret Martin. Building Vocabulary, Vol. A, B, C.
Lincolnwood, IL: National Textbook Co., 1981.

———. English Across the Curriculum, Vol. 1, 2, 3. Lincolnwood, IL:
National Textbook Co., 1983.

Murphey, Tim. "Teaching for Peak Relevance Using International
Pop Music." TESOL Newsletter 19.6 (December 1985): 13.

 Procedure

1. The bibliography for a paper or book should contain information about every source the author used in writing the paper or book. As you do your research, keep a record of the sources you use by making a bibliography card for each one. (See the previous chapter, "Taking Notes from Multiple Sources," for directions on how to make bibliography cards.)

2. Proofread your cards: be sure you have the correct spellings, dates, and other information for each source.

3. When you have finished writing your paper, put the bibliography cards for the sources you actually used in alphabetical order according to the last names of the authors.

4. Make a practice copy of your bibliography. Write or type *BIBLIOGRAPHY* at the top of the page in the center. Make an entry for each source, following the formats given below and in the **Example** for various types of sources. Be sure the entries are in alphabetical order. Look at the **Example** for help.

5. Follow this format to make an entry for a book:

a. Put the author's last name first, followed by a comma and his or her first name. Put a period after the author's first name. Then type the title of the book and underline it. Put a period after the title.

Blosser, Betsy. <u>Living in English.</u>

b. Next, put the publisher's city (and the state, if it's not a major city). It's all right to abbreviate the name of the state. Separate the city from the state with a comma. Put a colon after the state (or after the city, if the state isn't shown).

Lincolnwood, IL:

c. Type the name of the publisher and the date of publication next. Use a comma to separate the publisher from the date of publication. Put a period after the publication date. That is the end of the entry.

National Textbook Co., 1989.

d. If the book has more than one author, list the authors' names in the order they appear in the book. Follow these formats:

Jones, Kate, and Elizabeth Grimm.   (two authors)

Casey, Robert, J. D. Thompson, and Paula Locke.   (three authors)

DeMar, Letitia, et al.   (more than three authors)

e. If no author is given for the book, start the entry with the title and alphabetize it by the first word (other than *a, an,* or *the*) in the title.

6. Follow this format to make an entry for a magazine or journal article:

a. Put the author's last name first, followed by a comma and his or her first name. Put a period after the author's first name. Then type the title of the article and put a period after it. Put quotation marks (") before and after the title.

> Runnels, Curtis. "Greece Before the Greeks: The Neanderthals
> and Their Fate."

b. Type the name of the magazine or journal and underline it. Then put the volume number of the issue the article appeared in. If there's an issue number too, put a period after the volume number and add the issue number.

> Archaeology 42

> TESOL Quarterly 22.4

c. Next put the publication date in parentheses. Then put a colon followed by the page number(s) on which the article appeared. Put a period after the page number(s). This is the end of the entry.

> (March/April 1989): 43–47.

d. If the article has more than one author, list the authors' names as shown in step 5(d) above.

e. If no author is given for the article, start the entry with the title and alphabetize it by the first word (other than *a, an,* or *the*) in the title.

7. If you have more than one book or article by the same author(s) to list in your bibliography, put them in alphabetical order by title. You can save time and space by replacing the author's name with three hyphens in each entry after the first one.

Raudsepp, Eugene. How Creative Are You? New York: The Putnam
      Publishing Group, 1981.

---. More Creative Growth Games. New York: The Putnam
      Publishing Group, 1980.

8. If you need to make an entry for a source other than a book or a magazine or journal article, refer to a stylebook such as the *MLA Handbook for Writers of Research Papers*, second edition, by Joseph Gibaldi and Walter S. Achtert (New York: The Modern Language Association of America, 1984). The *MLA Handbook* contains detailed instructions and examples of bibliography entries for many different types of sources.

9. Proofread your bibliography. Then type a final copy and proofread it.

10. Put your bibliography at the end of your paper. It should be the last page of your work.

 Practice

Now it's your turn.

TASK: to write a bibliography

SITUATION: You have been asked to write a paper about emigration laws. The first thing you have to do is to read what the emigration laws are for different countries. Since you are going to do the bibliography only, and will not actually write the paper now, choose three or four countries whose emigration laws interest you. Go to the library and look for sources that tell about the emigration laws of these countries. Remember to take index cards with you so you can make a bibliography card for each source you find. Prepare a bibliography of at least four books and/or articles on this subject.

Did you remember to

1. put your sources in alphabetical order?
2. include all the necessary information? (See the **Procedure**.)
3. use the correct punctuation?
4. type or write your bibliography on unlined paper?
5. proofread?

CHAPTER 21
Writing a Term/ Research Paper

Some high school teachers and most college professors ask students to write at least one long paper for their classes. Students are usually given several weeks or even months to work on these papers. They're not hard to do, and they can be very interesting for the writer as well as for the reader. Research papers take time and care, but with the right attitude and materials, you can learn a great deal and earn a grade to be proud of.

 Rationale

Writing a term paper or research paper will give you practice in developing many skills and will help you learn more about a certain topic. Because of the limited time available in the classroom, teachers can't always teach as much as they would like about every subject. If you research a topic on your own, you will learn about the subject in more depth. Also, your *active* participation in the learning process will help you remember what you've learned.

 Materials Needed

$3'' \times 5''$ or larger index cards, pens and pencils, several sources containing information on your topic, typewriter or word processor, unlined paper for typing, composition paper

 Skills Involved

locating sources; gathering information; recognizing important material; taking and organizing notes; using correct grammar, punctuation, and spelling; writing sentences and paragraphs in an interesting and organized way; using footnotes; creating a bibliography

If you are asked to choose your own topic, another very important skill you will learn is how to narrow a topic to one that is appropriate for a term paper.

▷▷ Important Vocabulary

appropriate right, suitable

attitude a way of feeling or behaving

author writer

bibliography a list of sources appearing at the end of a book, article, research paper, or other reading. It tells the title, author, publisher, publication date, and pages for each source.

footnote a note placed at the bottom of a page to explain or give more information about something on the page, such as the source of the material. When you see a raised number at the end of a sentence, you should look at the bottom of the page for a *footnote*.

footnoting making a footnote, often to tell the source of an idea or fact

index cards small white cards, usually lined on one side and unlined on the other. The most common size is $3'' \times 5''$ (three inches by five inches).

in more depth in more detail, more thoroughly

limited kept to a certain amount, restricted

narrow a topic focus on a specific part of a topic

organizing putting things in order

publisher a company that prepares, prints, and sells books, magazines, or other written materials

research searching (looking) for and reading information from many sources about a particular topic

research paper a paper of several pages that usually deals with one subject in depth and is based on information gathered through research

source a person, place, or object that contains information

taking notes writing down in abbreviated form what you want to remember from something you're reading or hearing

term paper a paper on a particular subject, usually due near the end of a school term. A term paper usually requires research and has footnotes and a bibliography.

title the name of a book, speech, play, or other work

topic subject

 Example

See Appendix D for a sample term paper.

Procedure

1. Choose a topic and narrow it down to something realistic. You don't want your topic to be too general. For example, entire books have been written about the lives of famous people. If you want to write a term paper about a famous person, you will have to narrow your topic by focusing on one part of that person's life. If you want to write about the effects of war on people's lives, you will have to choose certain wars and the people and countries who were affected by them, rather than trying to write about all wars. Otherwise, your information would be too general and your paper would be too long. Your topic should give you an idea for a title for the paper.

2. Go to the library and use the vertical files, card catalog or on-line catalog, and *Reader's Guide to Periodical Literature* to find sources for your paper.

3. Take notes as you read each source, following the procedure described in the chapter on "Taking Notes from Multiple Sources," pages 158–177.

4. When all your notes are written on index cards, group them by putting together the cards from different sources that contain information about the same subject. For example, if you are writing about the way teenagers dressed in the 1950s, you might put all your cards about hairstyles in different parts of the world in one pile, all your cards about leather jackets in another pile, etc. Or you might group your cards by country, so you could talk about the styles in one country at a time. Since your notes are on individual cards, they are easy to work with. The important thing is to organize them so they will make sense to the reader.

5. Make an outline for your paper, following the directions on pages 119–123.

6. Write an introduction for your paper. The introduction is the first part of a paper. It tells what the purpose of your paper is—why you

are writing on this particular subject. It leads the reader into the
information you have put together from your notes.

An introduction for a paper on the history and development of the
short story, for example, might sound something like this:

Short Stories and You[1]

For as long as there have been people, there have been stories

about people. From our earliest beginnings, human beings have

been curious about each other and have satisfied that curiosity with

myths, legends, adventure tales, fantasy—stories. People respond to

stories that have a special enduring quality—a sparkle of life, a bit

of truth, a glimpse of ourselves.

7. After you have written your introduction, go back to your note
cards and make sure you've organized them well. Write your paper,
working with your cards in order and adding sentences that will make
your paper interesting and easy to understand. This will be a *rough
draft* or *practice copy* that you can read and correct and rewrite until
you've expressed everything as well as you can.

8. As you write your paper, be sure to tell where you got the
information you are using. One way to do this is by footnoting. In
general, you should make a footnote for each piece of information you
use that is not common knowledge.

A footnote tells the name and author of the source in which you
found a piece of information, plus all the other information a
bibliography entry for that source would include. (See pages 181–183.)
A footnote also tells the page or pages on which the information
appears in the book or article. Below are examples of the format you
should follow when making a footnote for a book or magazine article:

[1]Betsy J. Blosser, <u>Living in English</u> (Lincolnwood, IL: National ——— book
Textbook Co., 1989) 122.

[2]Charles E. Cobb, Jr., ''Living with Radiation,'' <u>National</u> ——— magazine article
<u>Geographic</u> 175.4 (April 1989): 411–12.

---

[1]John S. Simmons and Malcolm E. Stern, *The Short Story and You* (Lincolnwood,
IL: National Textbook Co., 1986) vii.

As you write your paper, whenever you include a piece of information that is not common knowledge—and *especially* when you use a direct quote from someone else—put a raised number at the end of the sentence containing that information. Then, at the bottom of the page, make a footnote with the same number that tells where you got the information. Number the first footnote in your paper number 1, and continue numbering your footnotes in order throughout your paper.

If you prefer, and if your teacher permits, you can use endnotes in your paper instead of footnotes. Endnotes contain the same information, follow the same format, and are numbered the same way as footnotes. The only difference is that they are placed together at the end of the paper, just before the bibliography, instead of at the bottom of each page. See Appendix D, pages 215–217, for an example.

After you have made one footnote or endnote for a particular source, any additional notes for that same source can be shortened to include only the author's last name and the page or pages on which the information appeared:

[3]Blosser 74–75.

However, if you are using two or more sources by the same author, you must include the title of the book or article, too:

[4]Blosser, <u>English for Adult Living</u> 39.

For more information and examples of footnotes and endnotes for different types of sources, refer to a stylebook such as the *MLA Handbook for Writers of Research Papers*, second edition, by Joseph Gibaldi and Walter S. Achtert (New York: The Modern Language Association of America, 1984).

9. Type your paper on unlined paper.

10. Put your bibliography cards in alphabetical order and prepare your bibliography, following the directions in "Writing a Bibliography," pages 180–183.

11. Type your bibliography and put it at the end of your paper.

12. Be sure your pages are in order. Number them at the bottom of the page, beginning with page 2.

13. Proofread your final copy and correct any mistakes before giving the paper to your teacher.

▶ Practice

Now it's your turn.

TASK: to write a term/research paper

SITUATION: Your teacher has asked you to write a term paper. You can choose your own topic. Remember to follow the directions in the chapters on "Making an Outline," "Taking Notes from Multiple Sources," and "Writing a Bibliography." You have a lot of work to do, but if you follow the directions it will be easy and rewarding. Before you begin, reread the list of "Materials Needed" for this chapter. You will need to use your own paper for this Practice.

APPENDICES

Appendix A

(Transcript of a telephone call for use in Practice, "Taking a Message." See page 21.)

YOU: Hello.

CALLER: This is Mrs. Sung. Let me speak to Mr. Patel, please.

YOU: I'm sorry. Mr. Patel isn't here right now. Can I take a message?

CALLER: Yes. I ordered three cans of cola and two gallons of milk. He sent me two cans of cola and three gallons of milk. I want him to send me the correct order. I can't come to the store because my baby is sick.

YOU: Hold on a minute, please. How do you spell your name?

CALLER: S-U-N-G.

YOU: Is that *F* as in *Frank?*

CALLER: No, *S* as in *soda.* S-U-N as in Nancy-G.

YOU: Okay, Mrs. Sung. Now, what is the correct order?

CALLER: Three cans of cola and two gallons of milk. He sent me . . .

YOU: Okay, Mrs. Sung. I'll give Mr. Patel the message. I'm sure he'll correct the mistake. Where do you live?

CALLER: I live right next door in apartment 14L.

YOU: Can I have your telephone number, please?

CALLER: 555-8797.

YOU: 555-8797. Mr. Patel will take care of it as soon as he comes back.

CALLER: Thank you. I hope he gets back soon.

YOU: Good-bye, Mrs. Sung.

Appendix B

(Transcript of a lecture on taking tests for use in Practice, "Taking Notes from a Lecture." See page 148.)

Do you know how to take a test? When you take a test, you must know the information on the test. You must also know how to take the test. It is important to understand the directions and follow them.

Some tests don't ask you to write information. They ask you to decide if something is correct or not correct. These are often called "true or false" tests. Some tests ask you to decide which answer is correct. You must choose the correct answer from two or three possible answers. These are "multiple choice" tests.

Some tests ask you to put two parts of an answer together. Usually one part of the answer is on the left side of the paper and the other part of the answer is on the right side of the paper. These are "matching" tests. Some tests have sentences with a missing word or words. Sometimes the missing words are listed and you must write them in the correct places. Sometimes there are more words listed than you need, and you must decide which ones to use. Sometimes there are no words listed. Then you must think of the missing words and write them in. These are all called "fill-in" tests. Sometimes you have to answer the questions on a test by writing all the information in paragraph form. This is called an essay test.[1]

---

[1]Some of the material for this lecture is taken from *English Across the Curriculum 2,* by Margaret Martin Maggs (Lincolnwood, IL: National Textbook Co., 1982, pages 21–28).

Appendix C

(Example of a paper written using notes from many sources. See "Taking Notes from Multiple Sources," page 172.)

AN AMERICAN FAMILY IN JAPAN

Planning to move to Japan? There are many cultural and educational differences you should be aware of to make life easier for you and your family.

If you have children, you should know that the educational system is different in many ways, although the system is divided by years much the same way as it is in the United States. Education is free in Japan the first nine years and is compulsory through ninth grade.[1] Students from other countries need a special visa via a note of authenticity from the school they are attending to verify they are actively engaged in study.[2] This is in addition to the special visa that you will need to come to Japan to live and work. Private schools with American curricula are available in the big cities at high prices.

When the American Occupation took over Japanese schools in 1945, they eliminated shushin or "moral education."[3] The Japanese taught morality based on the Confucian concept that "success in life is determined by academic achievement and respect for the rights of others."

---

[1]Theodore F. Welch and Hiroki Kato, Japan Today! (Lincolnwood, IL: Passport Books, 1986) 28.

[2]Edward A. Schwarz and Reiko Ezawa, Everyday Japanese (Lincolnwood, IL: Passport Books, 1988) 163.

[3]Boye De Mente, The Japanese Influence on America (Lincolnwood, IL: Passport Books, 1989) 161.

Japanese students attend school for 240 days each year. Juku, or supplementary schools, exist to help students prepare for college entrance tests, which are very difficult.

There are sixteen different statuses for visitors to Japan. Visitors must carry their passports at all times. Visas are needed and a letter of guarantee is required for foreigners who want to stay a long time. This should be prepared by a Japanese individual or organization who will promise to assist the foreigner if he or she has financial or other problems. If you are a foreigner employed in Japan, you must obtain a letter of employment showing the period of employment and how much you will be earning. If you are not employed, you may have to show how you will support yourself.[4]

Business practices are very different in Japan, and many Americans lose "deals" because they don't understand the culture. For example, the American businessman usually tells everything he has to say and expects the Japanese to do the same. The Japanese businessman, on the other hand, will sit back and listen and not say anything, sometimes for a very, very long period of time. The American gets nervous and starts talking too much and making concessions. The more he talks, the quieter the Japanese gets. He is a very shrewd negotiator. He also does little business with women.[5] That is another story.

Japanese society is vertical; it is based on superior/

---

[4]Schwarz and Ezawa 162.

[5]Boye De Mente, How to Do Business with the Japanese (Lincolnwood, IL: Passport Books, 1987) 101.

subordinate relationships.[6] When you walk into a Japanese office, you know what rank a person holds by where he or she is sitting. The closer a person sits to the door, the lower his or her rank is. The first introduction between businessmen is not a handshake but the presentation of the Name Card, like our business card, which tells the person's name, rank, and company. Bilingual cards are handed Japanese side up, with both hands and a slight bow. You are treated according to your rank after your card has been presented and read.[7]

Wa, or "circle," stands for the mutual trust between manager and laborer. There is loyalty, mutual responsibility, job security, collective responsibility for decisions and results, and no competitive pressure. There also is no fooling around in the workplace.[8]

The Japanese mix business and pleasure and do a lot of entertaining outside the home. Women are traditionally not included and this makes for some very lonely American wives. If wives do not speak Japanese, they often suffer from feelings of isolation in the tremendously crowded atmosphere where they never can forget they are foreigners.[9] Much time is spent getting their children to and from school since they must provide their own transportation and since driving in Japan is a very different experience.

Japanese drive on the left side of the road as people do

---

[6]Boye De Mente, Japanese Etiquette and Ethics in Business (Lincolnwood, IL: Passport Books, 1987) 22.

[7]De Mente, Japanese Etiquette and Ethics in Business 28.

[8]De Mente, Japanese Etiquette and Ethics in Business 37.

[9]De Mente, How to Do Business with the Japanese 239.

in England. If you have a driver's license from the United States, you can get a license in Japan, but if you have to get a license for the first time, that is a time- and money-consuming experience. Before you can get a license, you have to take a mechanics test to prove your knowledge of engines and how to repair them.[10] You must attend a government-regulated driving course that includes five hours on the construction and operation of a motor vehicle as part of twenty-five hours of classroom lectures. You have to practice dry runs on a simulator and have seventeen sessions at the wheel on a driving range with an instructor. Then you receive a learner's permit, which allows you to drive on selected roads and streets. After completing ten hours of off-range driving in designated areas and spending about $1,500 for the course, you can try for your driver's license. There is no place on the license for the color of a person's hair or eyes because Japan is such a homogeneous country.[11]

Finding a place to live in Japan is also an experience for the American. Housing can be very expensive. Besides having to pay one or two months' rent plus a security deposit before moving in, there is also a nonrefundable "thank you money" gift given to the landlord. Flush toilets should not be taken for granted when renting or buying a home. Japanese room size is measured by the number of tatami mats in the room. Tatami mats are the typical floor covering in a Japanese house. As a sanitary measure, shoes

[10]De Mente, How to Do Business with the Japanese 248.

[11]De Mente, How to Do Business with the Japanese 249.

are never worn inside the house. They would bring in dust and dirt that would get on the tatami mats. There is a special alcove where shoes are kept when not in use.[12] Futons, bed rolls, are rolled up and put away when they are not in use for sleeping. A guest of honor in the house is always given a special seat in front of the takonoma, an alcove.

Very little entertaining is done in the home. When you go to a restaurant, you are given wet cloths when you sit down—hot in winter, cool in summer. Japanese often tip in advance to ensure good service. Tips are given not to the employees but to the hotel or restaurant to help defray the cost of benefits to the employees. Good service is expected. Tips are not expected by employees and are forbidden in some places. Party participants are expected to be part of the entertainment during a gathering in a restaurant or night club.[13]

Below is some other interesting general and cultural information for the non-Japanese:

Communal baths are still a part of Japanese life. However, people are expected to wash before they get into the tub, whether at home or at a hotel. One is expected to be clean when entering a communal tub, where the water is not changed with each group of bathers.[14]

There are still a lot of arranged marriages in Japan. Marriage services are provided by many large companies.

---

[12]De Mente, The Japanese Influence on America 139.

[13]De Mente, The Japanese Influence on America 148–149.

[14]Welch and Kato 11.

Japanese males at age thirty are pressured to marry by the companies they work for. Being single is a serious handicap to promotion.[15]

The Japanese celebrate many holidays we don't celebrate here; for example, Respect for the Aged Day, Adults' Day, Children's Day, Culture Day, Labor Thanksgiving Day, Doll's Festival, Girls' and Boys' Festivals, Festival of the Weaver, and many others. Japanese send New Year's cards the way we send Christmas cards. January 15 is set aside to honor the twenty-year-old: it is the day of legally becoming an adult.

Shinto is the indigenous religion of Japan. The word means "way of the gods." There is no one great figure of worship but rather a collection of beliefs and ideas about the proper way of behavior that have developed over two thousand years.[16]

The tea ceremony is very special. The host and guests have special formal roles. The ceremony takes time to learn. For example, pocket paper is used by guests to place wagashi or Japanese cake on, or to wipe the tea bowl dry after drinking tea.[17]

Finally, knowing something about Japanese telephone booths can really help. There are different colors for different calls. Blue is for any distance; tall red booths are for long distance; short red booths are for local calls; and yellow booths are especially good for long distance.[18]

---

[15]De Mente, The Japanese Influence on America 157.

[16]Schwarz and Ezawa 128–129

[17]Schwarz and Ezawa 96.

[18]Schwarz and Ezawa 62.

There are many good books to read on the life and
culture of Japan. We suggest those in the bibliography as a
good start.

Appendix D

(Example of a term paper. See "Writing a Term/Research Paper,"
page 188.)

THE AMISH
By Kathy Blattner
Richwoods High School

THE AMISH

Even though we live in a highly technological society, there is a group of people who live successfully resistant to change, modern conveniences, fads, world crisis, or social status. This group is the Amish.[1]

In 1693 in Europe, Jacob Ammann led a group of people to form a group separate from the Mennonites. The group became the Amish, taking their name from their leader.[2] The Amish are a plain religious group that has maintained many of the same beliefs as the Mennonites, although the Amish do follow their beliefs more strictly.[3]

The Amish wanted to come to America to escape from the persecution they suffered in Europe. While in Europe, they were not allowed to buy or even rent land; and they were often heavily taxed. They were not allowed to live together in a community and therefore were unable to be a close group.[4]

The Amish began to come to America early in the 1700s. Within one hundred years, they were almost nonexistent in Europe, having either left or merged again with Mennonite churches. An invitation from William Penn to the Amish brought many to the colony of Pennsylvania. Soon they spread to other areas of the new country and established communities and congregations.[5]

In their early years in Europe, the Amish were persecuted for their beliefs. As a result, they held their church services in homes. Every other Sunday, the Amish still meet for worship in the home of one of the congregation.[6] Only the members of the congregation know whose home the service will be in.[7] They sit on hard benches that are moved from house to house. Their homes are designed to hold the congregation by opening up smaller rooms to make one large room.[8] The sermon, worship, and singing of hymns are done in German,[9] and it might last from three to four hours.[10] Following the worship service, dinner is enjoyed by the entire group.[11]

A special congregational meeting called an Ordnungsgemee is held twice a year to make the rules that become the Ordnung. These rules set down the way an Amish person lives. All members of the congregation know the Ordnung. The older rules of the Ordnung have been printed. These rules apply mainly to the principles of separation, apostasy, nonresistance, and exclusion. It is usually the borderline issues that are discussed by the congregation at the meeting. The issues of contemporary nature and those that apply only to a specific congregation continue to be unwritten.[12]

The Ordnung clarifies what is sinful or worldly. Many of the rules are based on Biblical passages; however, some have no Biblical support. These rules are justified by saying that it would be worldly to do otherwise. It is important for the Amish to maintain their separation from the world, and the congregation must agree on how to remain separate. The meetings held twice a year provide the time for the members to declare their unity toward issues.[13]

Excommunication from the church is the punishment given an Amish person accused of disobeying the Ordnung. The offender is warned and is expelled only after he refuses to change. The wrong behavior may be living openly in sin, causing divisions among the Amish, or teaching false doctrines. Specific examples of wrong behavior that could lead to excommunication are buying a car, talking to an excommunicated person, disobeying the dress code, or arguing with another person.[14]

When an Amish person is expelled from the church, the Ordnung calls for the congregation to practice Meidung. This is a shunning and calls for avoiding association with the excommunicated person.[15] "The Biblical instruction is that one neither 'eat' with such a person nor 'keep company' (I Cor. 5:11)."[16]

A person may be pardoned and become a part of the congregation once again if he acknowledges his sins and makes amends. If it is a minor offense, he needs to make only a formal apology to the church. However, if the offense is major, he needs to have the welcome of the bishop after confessing to the wrong on his knees. The fear of being shunned by their family and friends keeps some Amish from disobeying the Ordnung.[17]

An Amish person is not born Amish. All men and women must decide themselves if they want to become

3

Amish. If they do, they are baptized into the church.[18] The vow of baptism is an expression of faith, so it can be given only to those old enough to understand and pledge their faith.[19] They realize that to become Amish means to live by the rules of the church. This affects the entire life style of a person since religion and everyday life are intertwined.[20]

A very special occasion in the life of the Amish is the birth of a child. Each child born into an Amish family is felt to be a gift of God.[21] Amish children are a very important part of the community. No child is ever unwelcome. A newborn child brings happiness to the family and community since he will enlarge their Amish society. Children also mean more church members and workers.[22]

For the first two years of an Amish child's life, he is given everything he wants. After that, the parents begin to discipline the child.[23] Children receive ''on-the-spot'' discipline from their relatives because they work closely and almost continuously together.[24] An Amish child will soon learn that he is ''different'' from ''English'' children, but he will learn to take pride in his difference and follow his parents' example. Children are raised with such great amounts of love and care that they never feel secure outside their community.[25]

Marriage in an Amish community means that a couple is ready to move from youth and adolescence to adulthood. Courting is kept secret. The majority of the community will not know of an intended wedding until it is announced in

4

church. Close friends of a potential bride or groom often look for signs of an upcoming wedding. An overabundance of celery growing in the garden of the potential bride is considered a sign, since large amounts of celery are used at weddings. When the father of a potential bridegroom tries to buy extra land, it is also considered a sign of an upcoming wedding. When a young man is ready to be married, he tells his minister, and the minister talks to the bridegroom's intended fiancée. He verifies her wish to be married and obtains the consent of her parents. The intent of the couple to be married is later announced or "published" during a church service.[26]

Another major occurrence in the lives of the Amish, although not as happy as marriage, is death. Death is a natural part of life to the Amish. The Amish live to "store treasures" in heaven instead of accumulating material goods. The relatives do grieve, but they do not have a long period of mourning. Remembering the person and his role in life is emphasized. The process of preparing for a funeral is a community project. Someone makes the coffin when it is needed, and the burial site is prepared while the family and friends prepare the body. Some communities have bodies embalmed, although many do not. The tasks of running the home and farm are taken over by friends until the funeral is over. There is no payment to anyone for services. The body is usually kept in the home and someone sits with the dead day and night. The funeral is held on the third day after

5

death. The theme is usually centered around the Biblical theme, "The Lord giveth and the Lord taketh away." The cemetery is small and people are not buried in family plots but in the order they die. The marker is made by another community member and gives only the name and dates of birth and death.[27]

The simplicity shown in handling the death and funeral of an Amish person is also shown in their homes. They are very plain and simple and there are no decorative items. There may be a few plants and a calendar, but no pictures, mirrors, or knickknacks are allowed. The Amish must not use electrical appliances or bottle gas, and they are not allowed to have radios. These rules have been the same for years.[28]

The clothing worn by the Amish has also been the same style for years. Plainness and simplicity are important so no one looks or feels different from anyone else.[29] There may be slight differences in the way an Amish person dresses in separate Amish communities. These differences may seem small to an outsider, but they mean a lot to an Amish person.[30]

Amish women wear dresses that are completely alike. The dress pattern that they use has been handed down through the generations. Their dresses can be any solid color, but most women choose black, blue, green, or tan. A married woman always wears an apron that is either black or matches the color of her dress. An unmarried woman

6

always wears a white apron.[31] Little girls' dresses may have bright colors but may not have any pattern in the fabric.[32] Amish women must wear their "prayer caps" at all times. The caps are made of starched white organdy. They are worn on the back of their heads, and are tied under their chins in a small, neat bow.[33]

The clothing worn by men must not have buttons, because decorations of any kind on clothing are rejected entirely by Amish custom.[34] Also, since the Amish are pacifists, buttons are not used on clothing because they were originally used on military uniforms.[35] Men's hats are black and are made with specific regulations as to the size of the brim and the crown.[36] In most Amish communities, men are not allowed to wear neckties because they do not serve a useful purpose. A few communities, however, have allowed a narrow, black ribbon bow to be worn to church services and other dressy occasions.[37]

Just as the Amish have a uniformity in dress, they also have a uniform love and concern for one another. They provide support in times of trouble, so they do not need insurance coverage. In case of fire, the entire community will help rebuild the lost house or barn, contributing both materials and physical labor.[38] Although a community "barn-raising" becomes a social event, it is not planned as one. The Amish feel secure in knowing that in times of trouble, the other members of the church will help them. The spirit of fun and fellowship is always in the air at community gatherings. These feelings of security help the Amish in their daily work.[39]

The Amish farmer feels that the Bible tells him his job is to replenish the earth, till the soil, and have an abundant harvest. He loves the soil and works with it with care.[40] The farmer is not concerned with the highest possible yield per acre. He is mainly growing food for his family to eat, as well as feed for his animals. He is also concerned with preserving the soil, which he feels is a gift from God.[41] Rules governing farming are a part of the Ordnung also. In most Amish communities, all of the farm equipment must be horse-drawn.[42] One advantage for the farmer when using horses rather than a tractor is his ability to hear and observe the wildlife around him.[43]

Even though most Amish men are farmers, each community has some businessmen who make the items necessary for use in homes and farming. There are those who make buggies, caskets, farm machinery, and household furniture.[44] Some shops needed by an Amish community are a blacksmith and a harness shop.[45] The Amish are the major manufacturers of buggies, which are very expensive.[46]

Before joining their chosen trade or profession, each Amish girl and boy attend school for eight years. They attend one-room schools with all grades together, and their teacher probably has only an eighth-grade education herself if she is Amish. Some states are demanding that the teachers be certified; therefore, the teacher may be non-Amish in

8

some communities. The Amish are struggling with this change forced on them and are forming Amish parochial school programs. It is considered unnecessary and worldly for a student to go to high school. Instead, the girls are taught to care for a home, and the boys are taught the basics of farm management.[47]

Although the Amish do not have modern conveniences to help them with their daily work, their lives are not dull. Visiting friends and attending auctions are just two of the things that the Amish do to keep busy. Sewing and quilting provide a chance for the women to talk, and even the big job of harvesting is fun when a lot of friends work together.[48]

Children also have many ways of having fun after they have finished their chores. They have homemade toys, and they enjoy many games.[49] Popping corn and pulling taffy are just two of the things that Amish children and teenagers do at "sings." They also provide the older boys with the chance to take their favorite girls home in their "courting buggies."[50] A favorite game among Amish men is chess. They often will even play against "English" (non-Amish) players. They are not, however, allowed to play cards.[51]

Although the Amish do not have much vacation time, visiting natural sites like the Grand Canyon and going to zoos are accepted since they are visiting gifts from God.[52]

> One family took their children to St. Louis and while there visited Forest Park Zoo. In commenting on the trip, the mother was amused, saying that her family proved to be about as much of an attraction at the zoo as the animals.[53]

9

The enjoyment of a Sunday afternoon drive is done in a horse-drawn buggy, since another modern convenience rejected by the Amish is the automobile. An unmarried man is apt to drive a one-seated buggy, while a family will have a two-seated one. One false belief most people have about the Amish is that they do not travel very often. The fact that the Amish have horses and buggies rather than automobiles does not keep them from traveling. Some Amish will hire a driver and his car to take them to a distant town for shopping. If most of the community is planning to go, someone may charter a bus. Each family will bring enough food to last them until they arrive at their destination. If they are going to be traveling for several days, they will stop at Amish communities along the way. At these communities, they will be fed and can spend the night. The Amish can travel all over the United States and never have to buy a meal or pay for a hotel.[54] "One Amishman, commenting on this practice, chuckled and said, 'We call that Mennoniting around!' "[55]

Very few Amish leave the faith. The closeness felt among the community members provides a bond that few want to break.[56] "Only about five per cent of the Amish break away."[57] The number of Amish in the United States has increased some over the years. This may seem strange since intermarriage is rare and seeking converts is not widely practiced. The reason for the increase would seem to come mainly from the common practice of having large families of

10

seven or more children. The children continue to abide by the traditions of generations before them.[58]

Although the Amish are separate from the rest of the world, they do not need to completely isolate themselves to remain stable. They do business in nearby non-Amish communities by trading their goods for items at stores. They are also allowed to seek medical care and other professional services.[59]

The Amish take pleasure in the simple things in their lives. Their interests in their homes, their community, their neighbors, and their hobbies keep them content.[60] The strongest bond that holds the Amish people together is their faith. Their belief that God has a personal interest in each life and each home and each community ties them tightly together.[61]

It has been over 275 years since the Amish first settled in America, but their customs and style of living have remained nearly the same.[62] As one Amish farmer said, "It is a satisfying life, not for everyone perhaps, but certainly for us."[63]

214·

ENDNOTES

[1]James A Warner and Donald M. Denlinger, The Gentle People (Soudersburg, PA: Mill Bridge Museum, 1969) 12–13.

[2]Philip Shriver Klein and Ari Hoogenboom, A History of Pennsylvania (New York: McGraw-Hill, Inc., 1973) 206.

[3]Millen Brand, Fields of Peace (Garden City, NY: Doubleday and Company, Inc., 1970) 32.

[4]Elmer Schwieder and Dorothy Schwieder, A Peculiar People: Iowa's Old Order Amish (Ames: The Iowa State University Press, 1975) 14–15.

[5]Schwieder and Schwieder 9, 16.

[6]Klein and Hoogenboom 441.

[7]John M. Zielinski, ''The Amish in Illinois,'' Adventure Road 14 (September 1978): 16–17.

[8]Brand 63.

[9]Klein and Hoogenboom 441.

[10]The Ohio Guide (New York: Oxford University Press, 1948) 394.

[11]Klein and Hoogenboom 441.

[12]John A. Hostetler, Amish Society (Baltimore: Johns Hopkins University Press, 1980) 84–85.

[13]Hostetler 84–85.

[14]Hostetler 86–89.

[15]Hostetler 86–89.

[16]Hostetler 86–89.

[17]Hostetler 86–89.

[18]Marc A. Olshan, ''Should We Live Like the Amish?'' Christianity Today 27 (February 4, 1983): 68.

[19]The Ohio Guide 394.

[20]Olshan 68.

[21]Warner and Denlinger 90.

12

[22]Hostetler 157.

[23]Hostetler 157–158.

[24]Merle Good and Phyllis Good, 20 Most Asked Questions About the Amish and Mennonites (Lancaster: Good Books, 1979) 57.

[25]Hostetler 157–158.

[26]Hostetler 191–192.

[27]Schwieder and Schwieder 34–35.

[28]Brand 63, 68.

[29]Brand 63.

[30]Hostetler 234–235.

[31]Elmer L. Smith, The Amish (Lebanon, PA: Applied Arts Publishers, 1973) 25.

[32]Brand 63.

[33]Smith 25.

[34]Brand 63–64.

[35]Warner and Denlinger 12.

[36]Brand 63–64.

[37]Smith 25.

[38]Brand 62.

[39]Smith 27.

[40]Warner and Denlinger 133.

[41]David Kline, "Amish Farming: The Gentle Way of Life," Saturday Evening Post 255 (March 1983): 62–63.

[42]Warner and Denlinger 108.

[43]Kline 62–63.

[44]The Ohio Guide 394–395.

[45]Paul M. Angle, ed., Illinois Guide and Gazetteer Chicago: Rand McNally and Company, 1969) 62.

[46]Brand 68, 71.

13

[47]Warner and Denlinger 44–45.

[48]Zielinski 17.

[49]Brand 58.

[50]Zielinski 17.

[51]Brand 58, 68.

[52]Schwieder and Schwieder 71–72.

[53]Schwieder and Schwieder 71–72.

[54]Schwieder and Schwieder 71–72.

[55]Schwieder and Schwieder 71–72.

[56]Brand 71.

[57]Brand 71.

[58]Klein and Hoogenboom 441.

[59]Schwieder and Schwieder 68–69.

[60]Cornelius Weygandt, The Plenty of Pennsylvania (New York: H. C. Kinsey and Company, Inc., 1942) 84.

[61]Good and Good 82.

[62]Warner and Denlinger 12–13.

[63]Kline 63.

BIBLIOGRAPHY

Angle, Paul M., ed. Illinois Guide and Gazetteer. Chicago:
    Rand McNally and Company, 1969.

Brand, Millen. Fields of Peace. Garden City, NY: Doubleday
    and Company, Inc., 1970.

Good, Merle, and Phyllis Good. 20 Most Asked Questions
    About the Amish and Mennonites. Lancaster: Good
    Books, 1979.

Hostetler, John A. Amish Society. Baltimore: Johns Hopkins
    University Press, 1980.

Klein, Philip Shriver, and Ari Hoogenboom. A History of
    Pennsylvania. New York: McGraw-Hill, Inc., 1973.

Kline, David. "Amish Farming: The Gentle Way of Life."
    Saturday Evening Post 255 (March 1983): 62–63.

The Ohio Guide. Compiled by workers of the Writers'
    Program. New York: Oxford University Press, 1948.

Olshan, Marc A. "Should We Live Like the Amish?"
    Christianity Today 27 (February 4, 1983): 68.

Schwieder, Elmer, and Dorothy Schwieder. A Peculiar People:
    Iowa's Old Order Amish. Ames: The Iowa State
    University Press, 1975.

Smith, Elmer L. The Amish. Lebanon, PA: Applied Arts
    Publishers, 1973.

Warner, James A., and Donald M. Denlinger. The Gentle
    People. Soudersburg, PA: Mill Bridge Museum, 1969.

Weygandt, Cornelius. The Plenty of Pennsylvania. New York:
    H. C. Kinsey and Company, Inc., 1942.

Zielinski, John M. "The Amish in Illinois." Adventure Road
    14 (September 1978): 15–17.